Praise for

can a te

What a great read! *What Else Can a Teacher Do?* should be read not only by all teachers who want a change, but also by all school leavers – including my 17-year-old daughter!

Kate Marnoch, Head Teacher, Kingsdown Nursery School, founding member, Lincolnshire Nursery Schools Partnership (LNSP)

Ideal for teachers feeling a bit dissatisfied with life and wondering where to start to change it, *What Else Can a Teacher Do?* offers fresh perspectives on reviewing where you're currently at and for thinking about yourself and your own needs (something we often find hard to do). The information provided on career opportunities is comprehensive, but it is the contemplation section which makes it stand out and makes it a worthwhile purchase.

An interesting, thought-provoking read.

Gordon Collins, owner, Gordon Collins Careers and Education Services

What Else Can a Teacher Do? is an interesting and reassuring book which considers the common issues that teachers (and other people) face during their careers. As a careers adviser myself I have spoken to many teachers who face and suffer the same issues, and I especially enjoyed the book's inclusion of comments from other people about their own experiences. The job profiles section is useful and gives readers the opportunity to consider themselves in other roles.

Paul Clifton, careers adviser

What else
can a teacher do?

Review your career, reduce stress and
gain control of your life

David Hodgson

Crown House Publishing Limited
www.crownhouse.co.uk

First published by
Crown House Publishing
Crown Buildings,
Bancyfelin,
Carmarthen,
Wales, SA33 5ND, UK
www.crownhouse.co.uk

and

Crown House Publishing Company LLC
PO Box 2223, Williston, VT 05495, USA
www.crownhousepublishing.com

British Library Cataloguing-in-Publication Data

A catalogue entry for this book is available from the British Library.

Print ISBN: 978-178583015-0
Mobi ISBN: 978-178583299-4
ePub ISBN: 978-178583300-7
ePDF ISBN: 978-178583301-4
LCCN 2017957030

Printed and bound in the UK by
Gomer Press, Llandysul, Ceredigion

Contents

Acknowledgements

I would like to thank the teachers who have contributed to this book: Jane Boyd, Rosemary Butcher, Stuart Swann, Alison Swann, Lucy Curtis, Kimberley Simms, Jason Batty, Steve Banbury and Kate Marnoch.

Their willingness to share their experiences with candour and modesty is both humbling and inspiring.

Many organisational websites – such as TARGETjobs, Prospects and the Higher Education Careers Services Unit (HECSU), which I frequently reference – are excellent sources of professionally produced careers information. I would also like to thank the Association of Graduate Careers Advisory Services (AGCAS) who have given me their permission to draw on online material produced by their hard-working careers advisers to inform this work.

The scariest moment is always just before you start.

Stephen King, *On Writing: A Memoir of the Craft*, p. 325
(on writing, but his words are equally applicable to anyone
considering a career change)

Introduction

As I watched another repeat of *QI* on Dave I remembered the quote attributed to Seneca: 'It is not that we have a short time to live, but that we waste a lot of it.' Time is precious and limited. We owe it to ourselves to make the most of it. A common way to waste it is staying in the wrong job. The only way to live fully is to be in the right job for you.

I work in schools, colleges and universities across the UK and abroad with teachers and students. Every day I witness the unique exhilaration of the teacher's role. It really can be both the most rewarding and frustrating job in the world, bringing unexpected joy and unbearable agony, often in the same lesson.

I regularly meet teachers who are pondering their career options. Staying in any job is ultimately the wrong choice when your heart or head isn't in it. This is especially the case in teaching, where coasting or ploughing along is not a healthy option.

This book presents some other options. I meet so many teachers who have found ways to fulfil their potential and fully utilise their talents, some by making seemingly small adjustments, such as a change of school (sometimes in a different country), and others by taking a complete change of direction and never looking back. Some even leave and then return to teaching following a brief flirtation with the so-called real world, reinvigorated and bursting with relevant experiences to boost their teaching.

Whether or not you make small or major changes, I hope you'll find this book useful. I have spoken to many teachers who have been candid about their own journey, and have included some of their comments. Common themes include a passion and commitment for their chosen vocation, a slow erosion of this passion due to an unbearable workload or lack of support 'from above', an exploration of their options based on their contacts or broader interests, and discovering a niche within or outside education. This book is not meant to be a survival guide or an escape manual. A survival guide implies you'll do just enough frenetic gasping and paddling to keep your head above the turbulent waves. But you deserve more. I've included plenty of suggestions in an effort to help you improve your current position. The right small change may be enough to get you through a difficult time and on to the next stage of your teaching journey. An escape manual is an equally dangerous proposition. It implies that change is easy. It is not. Some alternatives to teaching are laid out so you can take a peek with a dispassionate and critical eye if you are contemplating making a bigger change in your working life.

Advice from teachers

'Will I still be sitting in this chair thirty years from now?'

The government initiative Languages for All meant I went from living in France and studying French literature to teaching French to children on Tyneside, who hated the subject and culture as much as I loved it. It was so wearing. The lesson in which pupils role played buying a postage stamp in a French post office to send to Austria was a memorable low point. As I sat in the staffroom afterwards, I had an eerie premonition: will I still be sitting in this chair thirty years from now? I knew I needed a change, but wasn't sure *what* change. Counselling appealed to me, so I decided to do supply teaching part-time and train as a counsellor in the evenings. I soon realised I would be rubbish as a counsellor, because I didn't have the patience to listen to people's problems without jumping in with a solution. The only part of the course that gripped me was psychology, so I signed up for an Open University degree in psychology and studied for four years. At the same time, I was teaching part-time in a school that was developing its sixth form. I was asked if I would like to set up a department and teach psychology. Three years later I moved to a sixth form college, where I still work. I enjoy the energy and commitment of the staff and students here. The subject still fascinates me, but we all work too hard and are swamped by constant change, which makes things more difficult. I never really planned my career properly, but moving around within teaching has been better for me than staying put.

Jane

Part 1 of this book lists some statements you need to consider as you decide whether or not to:

- stay in teaching
- tweak your role to move into a different educational position, or
- make a complete break and move in another direction completely.

After thinking about these statements and completing the activities, you will hopefully identify your best next step. No decision is irreversible. Many teachers return to the classroom later in their career, boosted by a new set of skills, experiences and confidence.

Part 2 of the book explores your options in and around teaching. There are at least thirty career moves you can make which all retain teaching at their core. Some are relatively straightforward, like teaching different classes or moving to a different school, and others are more exotic – teaching on film sets, in hospitals or creating teaching resources for the stage version of Disney's *The Lion King*. This includes a section for teachers relatively new to the profession, who could leave and compete for graduate-entry careers. Part 2 ends with a section highlighting options for senior teachers.

Part 3 presents some more dramatic options in the form of a list of around 120 careers. They are meant to show the wide range of jobs available. Some require minimal or no further training, while others demand a lengthy and expensive commitment. The jobs I have chosen all have some overlap with the skills and interests teachers develop in the classroom. In my role as a careers adviser, I worked with many teachers who decided to stay in education only after they had carefully examined and rejected the alternatives. Looking at Part 3 is not wasted time; it will help you to accurately compare your current position with some realistic career alternatives.

I worked as a careers adviser for over twenty years in County Durham. Secondary school teachers with a few years' experience were the most frequent visitors to the careers centres where I worked. They were often keen to sit down and explore their career options for an hour or two. Many other public sector workers were also curious to take a peek at their alternatives. I feel passionately that everyone should be supported to find a rewarding career that suits their unique mix of skills, qualities and experience, which is what prompted me to write this book. It is informed by the discussions I've had with teachers at various stages of their careers and the decisions they made; it addresses the most frequently asked questions that those teachers had as they searched for a clear career path that was right for them. I hope you'll find the answers you need here too.

Part 1

Where are you now?

In this section there are a number of statements to consider and checklists to complete. These will help you assess where you are now, and help you see where you're going more clearly. Write down your answers and any thoughts, either in the book or in a notepad. Do show all your working-out! As a teacher, you'll know how important it is to engage actively and reflect on the content rather than speed-read your way through it. You will not be externally assessed on your answers, but you will benefit from looking back over your responses to make sense of later sections.

In at the deep end?

Let's start by assessing where you are now.

Marilyn Clarke studied career patterns and identified four approaches adopted by staff facing a career transition.[1] Who are you?

Plodder: Focuses on present, loyal and hardworking. They pay little attention to personal career planning or networking.

Pragmatist: Focuses on a traditional career path within the prevailing organisational structure. They consider personal progression reactively as and when vacancies arise. Don't tend to update skills via additional training.

Visionary: Actively plan and execute their career plan and move employers to maintain control. Personally confident and proactive, undertaking additional training and opportunities.

Opportunist: Self-aware, they grasp opportunities and embrace change to continually develop new skills and knowledge. They demonstrate flexibility and are driven by their values.

Clarke concluded that adopting behaviours that promoted a future focus to career planning led to success. This book will help you develop these powerful habits through a series of steps starting with an exploration of your own strengths and values. You can then start to match these to the many career options available within and outside of teaching.

Successful teachers are likely to agree with most of the following twenty statements (pages 8–9). Have a look through them and see how you do. These beliefs can be developed, and this book will help embed these into your behaviour. If you're going to fill in the gaps, start with the lowest number first, as the list is in a logical order along the lines of: know yourself, develop a plan, then execute the plan. If you're competitive and want to

---

1   Marilyn Clarke, Plodders, pragmatists, visionaries and opportunists: career patterns and employability, *Career Development International* (2009) 14(1): 8–28.

score top marks and tick all the beliefs, then you can do so, but remember this isn't a test. It's a continuous improvement loop for life and your career. Even if you respond with a tick, you can consider additional action for that statement. If you make changes across a half a dozen or more, you will begin to notice a positive impact. Don't worry if you think this list seems a bit pushy and self-indulgent; John McEnroe might have said everybody loves success, but they hate successful people. The way to avoid this phenomena is to look *out*, not just in. Help friends and colleagues work on their progress, not just on your own, and nobody will begrudge you success. Perhaps one of the traps of the self-improvement movement is the descent into self-absorption and a focus on personal entitlement without offering genuine interest and support to those around us.

> According to an ATL survey, 83% of teachers have considered leaving the profession.[2]
>
> 40% of new teachers leave the profession within a year of qualifying.[3]

2   ATL, Workload drives the teacher recruitment and retention crisis, new survey finds (4 April 2016). Available at: www.atl.org.uk/media-office/2016/workload-drives-the-teacher-recruitment-and-retention-crisis.asp.

3   Sally Wheale, Four in 10 new teachers quit within a year, *The Guardian* (31 March 2015). Available at: www.theguardian.com/education/2015/mar/31/four-in-10-new-teachers-quit-within-a-year.

1 I know my skills and what I'm good at. ◯

....

2 I know the skills I need to develop. ◯

....

3 I can do an elevator pitch (a thirty-second summary of my ◯
  skills and best achievements to date, showcasing what I
  can add to an organisation or team).

....

4 I keep a record of all my major achievements at work. ◯

....

5 I seek regular feedback on my performance from colleagues ◯
  and students.

....

6 I share my ideas with other professionals. ◯

....

7 I take on new roles, projects or research at work to ◯
  enhance my skills and experience.

....

8 I feel good about myself at work. ◯

....

9 I know what opportunities for progression are available in ◯
  my current school.

....

10 I'm aware of the politics, tensions and 'characters' in my ◯
  current school.

....

11 I'm aware of the career options available to teachers in the UK and abroad. ○

....

12 I'm aware of the job options available outside teaching, and the entry routes for these options. ○

....

13 I have a pretty clear idea of my career direction, and what/ where I'd like to be in three years' time. ○

....

14 I have discussed my career plan with important people in my life. ○

....

15 I'm content with my life outside work. ○

....

16 I have a life outside work. ○

....

17 I have mentors. ○

....

18 I am articulate and assertive. ○

....

19 I keep up to date with what's going on by reading articles, blogs, journals, newspapers and books about education and my subject specialism. ○

....

20 I review and reflect on my progress. ○

....

Thinking more about where you are now

1 **I know my skills and what I'm good at.** You can learn how to develop these further. You can show that you have these qualities. The first part of this book will help you identify or clarify your main skills and strengths. This is how many teachers spot a new niche within the classroom or a different kind of space.

2 **I know the skills I need to develop.** You can develop a plan to help improve or gain these skills. Being able to learn from things that didn't go as well as we'd expected is fundamental to progress in life. We need to ask ourselves: what have I learned? What would I do differently? What can I do to make sure I do better next time? Can I find examples of this working well? Teachers encourage pupils to develop these meta-cognition and self-reflection skills, and they're just as important for adults. We all need to actively develop our strengths and skills to thrive.

3 **I can do an elevator pitch.** This is a thirty-second summary of your top skills and achievements to date, showcasing what you can add to an organisation or team. This is a good way to check that you are aware of who you are, what you have achieved and what you can contribute.

4 **I keep a record of all my major achievements at work.** This will help you create a strong CV, prepare for interviews and feel positive. It's human nature to forget the good stuff and dwell on the negative. However, try

focusing on the positive. What are your top three achievements from the past six months?

....

5 **I seek regular feedback on my performance from colleagues and students.** This can be informal and fun. Simply asking students to tell you something they liked about a lesson on their way out, or asking every fifth student for something that could be improved, provides quick feedback. This can build confidence and evidence for lesson observations from peers or inspectors. Offer genuine, positive and regular feedback to colleagues when you notice their great work in action. Don't wait to offer praise just before you ask them to do a favour for you; they could become suspicious of the preceding compliment.

....

6 **I share my ideas with other professionals.** This could be via TeachMeets, blogs, Twitter or courses. Connecting to like-minded people is really important, and will help embed these beliefs in your brain. Networking opportunities for teachers have grown over the past few years, and you can benefit from joining in real-life or online groups.

....

7 **I take on new roles, projects or research at work to enhance my skills and experience.** This could include quick and easy research with a class on which revision technique works best for a specific topic, an MA or anything in-between. You could become an exam marker to gain expertise and insights into how students answer questions in exams, and then run training for staff and students to share what you learned. This does not mean taking on everything in a scattergun manner. An elderly Malcolm Muggeridge said that one of the pleasures of old age is

giving things up. We can apply the same principle at work: consciously concentrate on the most important things (as identified in belief 2).

8 **I feel good about myself at work.** If we work hard and are doing the best we can, we should acknowledge this. We're not meant to be perfect. Reflect on what goes well, not only the bad days (see belief 4).

9 **I know what opportunities for progression are available in my current school.** This could be to gain more experience, learn from staff you admire, expand your skill base, complete training or have an eye on a promotion. If nothing comes to mind, could you start something new (aligned to your long-term aims)?

10 **I'm aware of the politics, tensions and 'characters' in my current school.** This doesn't mean you need to play Machiavellian games. The teachers who proclaim they avoid office politics at school are often the ones stuck in the middle of it, oblivious to the rolling eyes and damaging whispers of certain colleagues. To avoid it, you need to know what you're avoiding. As my wise dad said, 'You have to see the dog mess to avoid stepping in it.'

11 **I'm aware of the career options available to teachers in the UK and abroad.** It's not easy to keep up to date with all the opportunities in the education sector, because teaching is one of the largest and most valued professions across the world. However, if you make a conscious effort to explore your options, and adopt beliefs 6, 7 and 19, you will spot opportunities more often.

12 **I'm aware of the job options available outside teaching, and the entry routes for these options.** This book will enhance your awareness of your strengths and transferable skills, and how you could apply these in alternative careers.

13 **I have a pretty clear idea of my career direction, and what/where I'd like to be in three years' time.** This book is designed to help you with this. If you know what you'd like to be doing three years from now, go and talk to people who are already there. What did they do to get there? What advice/support could they offer? The clearer your vision regarding your progression, the better.

14 **I have discussed my career plan with important people in my life.** If you haven't, you're missing out on wisdom and insight from those who love you most. They'll generally offer encouragement and say, 'Great, go for it!' or help you in practical ways. If they disagree with aspects of your plan, then they could help you rectify or modify it.

15 **I'm content with my life outside work.** If there areas that need to be improved, start to list these and think about how you can work on them. Small steps are best. You have more control over things like health and fitness, whereas finding a new place to live or finding a partner may require a few more steps! One teacher once told me she realised she enjoyed teaching, but hadn't had a boyfriend for two years, and this was the thing she wanted to change. She liked men who played rugby so she took an evening job two nights a week in the bar at the local rugby club – to the dismay of some of her colleagues. She was basically auditioning boyfriend material. It worked. She found a partner and is now happier. This example is included

to remind us that it is worth considering your priorities beyond the classroom, and plan proactively to meet these. Many teachers find their life outside school shrinks due to the heavy workload. Sometimes they haven't noticed this happening until they've lost contact with friends and family and given up their hobbies and interests. This doesn't feature in the slick TV ads promoting teaching, but was mentioned by nearly every teacher I spoke to who had been in the classroom for five years or more.

....

16 **I have a life outside work.** Are you involved in satisfying social activities? Having friends and being socially connected seems to be a crucial ingredient for human health and happiness. Make sure you have hobbies and interests. This could be as simple as enjoying country walks or a lazy hour in a coffee shop. Allow yourself time to do something you know you enjoy.

....

17 **I have mentors.** This is in addition to friends, family and allocated line managers. You should have already identified people who can help you from earlier statements. If not, this is important. Successful people always say they couldn't have identified or achieved their goals without a mentor to help them with a timely piece of advice or encouragement. A teaching mentor is really valuable. This needs to be someone you choose and respect, not someone assigned as your mentor by someone else. That can sometimes work, but it is best to identify and approach your own mentors.

....

18 **I am articulate and assertive.** Developing the beliefs that precede this one will help you better promote and develop your identity at work and beyond it. Many teachers are modest, which is lovely in other contexts, but if we're not

objective and analytical about our own career path, our life can drift and wither. I've met many teachers aged over fifty who wished they could go back in time and make a different decision about what to do with their life.

....

19 **I keep up to date with what's going on by reading articles, blogs, journals, newspapers and books about education and my subject specialism.** Being curious about life is a trait of many successful people. Being knowledgeable about your work will help you spot and dismiss silly jargon, fads and initiatives that are worth avoiding, and focus on the niche that will help you contribute to your field in a meaningful and positive way. For example, research by the University of Durham and the Sutton Trust into what makes great teaching highlighted the importance of a teacher's deep subject knowledge and their ability to help pupils understand and ask good questions about their own knowledge.[4]

....

20 **I review and reflect on my progress.** This ensures you're on track and can make any necessary adjustments based on changes at work or in your private life.

....

---

4   Robert Coe, Cesare Aloisi, Steve Higgins and Lee Elliot Major *What Makes Great Teaching? Review of the Underpinning Research* (London: Sutton Trust, 2014). Available at: www.suttontrust.com/wp-content/uploads/2014/10/ What-Makes-Great-Teaching-REPORT.pdf.

The good, the bad and the ugly of teaching

Here is a summary of the good and bad of a classroom teacher's lot.

Positives

I'm my own boss

I'm working with a subject I love

I'm working with children

I can have a genuine and positive impact on the lives of children

I'm in a relatively secure job

I can be creative

I am never bored

I can make friends with like-minded colleagues

I have holidays at the best times

Negatives

I'm regularly physically and emotionally stretched and challenged

I can always find more stuff to do and can never relax

I'm working with difficult, and sometimes vulnerable, children and parents

I'm never going to get rich as a classroom teacher

I could easily get stuck in a rut or become cynical (without even knowing)

I will be working long hours and may be too tired to enjoy the holidays

Which of the previous statements ring true?

Keep them in the back of your mind as you read the following pages to help you reach a conclusion about what to do next. Ponder the following:

- Do the positives of your job outweigh the negatives?
- Can you reduce some of the negatives and develop the positives?

Of teachers considering leaving the profession, almost 90% cited 'heavy workload' as the main reason.[5] This is hard to avoid in most teaching jobs, and in most jobs generally. Some schools are aware of the negative impact of staff workload and the pressure it causes. Consider moving to such a school. To identify these enlightened schools, read their policies, talk to the senior leadership team (SLT) and compare teacher absentee rates and long-term sickness numbers.

Challenging pupil behaviour is the reason around one in four teachers leave a post. Could you move to other classes or roles to mitigate this? Moving to a school where challenging behaviour is less of an issue is a route taken by many of the teachers I've spoken to during the compilation of this book.

The Association of Teachers and Lecturers (ATL) reported that the other main factors are attacks on teachers' terms and conditions and constant teacher-bashing in the press; factors that are unlikely to change. If these are affecting you, it may be time to at least consider some of the more drastic alternatives in Part 3 of this book.

---

5   ATL, Workload drives the teacher recruitment and retention crisis, new survey finds (4 April 2016). Available at: www.atl.org.uk/media-office/2016/workload-drives-the-teacher-recruitment-and-retention-crisis.asp.

Everyone thinks they would be a great teacher. I remember the first time my husband read *The Very Hungry Caterpillar* to our son. As our cute toddler drifted off to sleep and my husband grew in confidence, emphasising h-u-n-g-r-y (reading at Key Stage 2, level 3), he must have thought he was a natural teacher, mentor and behavioural expert. He later asked me if I thought he'd be a good teacher. I told him to ask me after he'd read the story fifty times, had to improvise his own story, been randomly observed and assessed by an Ofsted inspector twice, prepared a lesson plan and test for it, displayed thirty caterpillar paintings on the wall, justified himself at parents' evenings for his choice of the book ... At this point he said, 'OK, I'll stay in accountancy.' I don't know why everyone thinks teaching is easy; they don't think the same about being a pharmacist, plastering or flying planes. Every time I see a smug politician do a staged reading in front of a group of hand-picked pupils, I wince and seethe in equal measure.

Anne

Are you growing, coasting or sinking in your current job?

Think about the statements below and tick the boxes that apply to you.

In class I'm still learning and improving my practice	or	I'm just applying what I already know
I am surprised and challenged, in a positive way, each day	or	I'm challenged, in a scary or draining way, each day
I regularly smile and laugh	or	I regularly feel sad during the day
I arrive home after work with positive anecdotes/stories to share about my day	or	I tend to arrive home and moan about the same people or problems each day
There are new projects/ideas I'd like to try out	or	There is no scope or desire for me to be innovative
I connect with new members of staff	or	I tend to stick with a few trusted colleagues
Outside the classroom, at school, I spend more time on activities that energise me	or	I spend more of my day on activities that drain me
I receive regular positive feedback from colleagues and students	or	I'm mostly picked up on things I've done wrong

▶ ○ More this   ○ bit of both   More this ○ ◀

More this side [left] These answers indicate you're thriving! You're making a positive contribution to the school and developing your skills and experience.

In the middle Most people have areas of their work that are good and areas in which they are coasting or struggling. The answers you have given will highlight which parts of the job are good and which areas need attention. Read on.

More this side [right] These answers indicate you may be sinking! This book should help you identify why and outline positive short- and long-term solutions.

The first five statements are about you and your internal state. The final three examine your school environment and the extent to which you are supported or undermined by the SLT.

Why do people leave a job?

It's not only teachers and people on TV talent shows who may be considering a career change. The most common reasons cited by people leaving all jobs are:

- I couldn't grow and develop my skills on the job or through training.
- I didn't have opportunities for career advancement, leading to higher earnings.
- The job did not use my talents.
- The job became boring.
- I couldn't see the positive end results of my work.
- I didn't receive regular constructive feedback on my performance.
- I didn't think the place I worked would recognise or reward my hard work.[6]

6   Leigh Branham, *The 7 Hidden Reasons Employees Leave: How to Recognise the Subtle Signs and Act Before It's Too Late* (New York: AMACOM, 2005).

These reasons are certainly relevant to teachers. They can be divided into two categories. First, personal: a mismatch between the job and your skills or ambitions. Second, environment: the school or leadership team is not providing appropriate support, feedback or training. Which of these apply to you? If it's environment, then a change of school or supervisor could be the solution, whereas if it's personal then a more drastic change is on the cards.

Patrick Lencioni suggests that there are three root causes of job misery: anonymity, irrelevance and immeasurability.[7] Experiencing any of these in your job can cause problems. Do you ever feel like this?

Anonymity

Do you feel invisible or isolated at work? Ironically, busy schools can be very lonely places for students and teachers.

Irrelevance

Do you feel you are not making a real difference? Are there too many obstacles in your way to achieving the things that attracted you to teaching in the first place? Can you see the positive impact of your contribution to students?

Immeasurability

Are you able to quantify your contribution? Can you tangibly measure your impact? Is helping students achieve target grades meaningful enough? For some teachers it may be satisfying to

---

7   Patrick Lencioni, *The Truth About Employee Engagement: A Fable About Addressing the Three Root Causes of Job Misery* (San Francisco, CA: Jossey-Bass, 2015).

watch their students make their journey through key stages, GCSEs, A levels, etc. Some students may not achieve this. Satisfied classroom teachers know this, and find a way to make an impact and measure it for each student they teach.

Ask experienced teachers what keeps them in the classroom year after year and they'll say it's the children. They find a way to connect with each student and understand what they need to do to help the student along their path (academic and/or personal). If there is a conflict between student needs and school/Ofsted needs, it is the teacher who feels lost or stuck in the middle who will begin to wilt.

Clues that it could be time to leave teaching

When work is making you ill

Recent physical or emotional illness is a big clue that work (or other important areas of your life, such as family or housing) needs your immediate attention. Have you been off work sick? Have your eating or drinking patterns radically changed? Do you feel a persistent anxiety as you arrive at school?

I've met teachers who cry in their cars for a few minutes before summoning up enough courage to enter the school; this means it is time to urgently assess your career choice, unless you can pinpoint the source to one person or class, in which case your response can be less drastic and more targeted.

A recent survey by *The Guardian*'s Teacher Network found that teachers' heavy workload is a major cause of stress.[8] One-third of teachers work more than sixty hours per week, and four out of five view their workload as unmanageable in the long term. Around seven out of ten teachers admit that work impacts negatively on their physical and mental health. If you are one of these teachers, you must do something about it – allowing the situation to continue can only harm yourself or others. Only one in eight teachers report a good work–life balance.

Some schools hint at a potential solution. Three Bridges School in London, which aims to be the happiest school in the world, reduced the amount of marking and written assessment given by teachers. The results have been positive, both lowering teacher stress and raising school results. The changes were introduced by Jeremy Hannay, a teacher from Canada who describes the system of high levels of accountability and scrutiny prevalent in England as a perfect way to improve the 10% of poorest-performing teachers, at the expense of stifling or driving away the other 90%.[9] Teachers who are given autonomy and allowed to be creative tend to thrive; this must surely apply to all professions. There are other schools with a similar ethos, though you may need to look for a while to find them.

American charter-school chain Knowledge is Power Program (KIPP) has identified three key ways to retain excellent classroom teachers: (1) providing meaningful recognition for their loyalty and excellence, (2) offering maximum autonomy and (3) being creative about advancement without the teacher having to leave the classroom. This is not rocket science, but very few schools actively nurture their greatest asset – staff.

8   Liz Lightfoot, Nearly half of England's teachers plan to leave in next five years, *The Guardian* (22 March 2016). Available at: www.theguardian.com/education/2016/mar/22/teachers-plan-leave-five-years-survey-workload-england.

9   Liz Lightfoot, Tips on reducing teacher stress from the 'happiest school on earth', *The Guardian* (22 March 2016). Available at: www.theguardian.com/education/2016/mar/22/teaching-crisis-school-what-keep-them.

Stress response checklist

Below are some of the symptoms you may feel if you're stressed. Are you suffering from any of these?

Body: Headaches, muscle tension/pain, chest pain, fatigue, sex-drive change, stomach upset, sleep problems.

Mood: Anxiety, restlessness, lack motivation/focus, irritability, anger, sadness.

Behaviour: Over-/undereating, angry outbursts, drug/alcohol abuse, social withdrawal.

The long-term effects of stress are even worse, so if you're suffering, read on and see where you can make positive changes.

In the short term, the following can help to reduce stress:

Exercising: Even a brisk thirty-minute walk every other day can have a positive impact on health and quality of sleep.

Mindful relaxation: Yoga, t'ai chi, a spa visit, massage and reading are all thought to benefit our mental health. Watching TV is the way most people say they relax, but it is debatable how effective this is.

Interests: Return to hobbies/interests you've let slip or try new hobbies.

Cultivate a positive outlook: List and ponder the things you are thankful for in your work and life. You don't have to become a watered-down version of a Buddhist monk, however. Although pessimism has been given a bad name, it's valuable to help us find a balanced view on the important matters.

Devote more time to friends/family/community: Researchers at Harvard University have studied over 700 people from different backgrounds since 1938, and discovered that good relationships predict happiness and health more than any other factor. It was the quality, not quantity, of strong relationships that mattered. It is possible to be lonely while you are surrounded by a thousand people in a school. Loneliness and exposure to high-conflict relationships kill: people exposed to high-conflict relationships die younger.[10]

Advice from teachers

I took up pottery to help me lower my high blood pressure. For three hours a week, I escaped from the grind of my teaching job. It was fantastic, even though the loft is full of ugly misshapen mugs and vases that would make Grayson Perry weep.

Paula

Five ways to be happier today

Listen to a favourite piece of music

Spend five minutes more with someone you like

Go outdoors

Help someone else

Have a new experience

Paul Dolan, speaking at the Hay Festival, 2015[11]

---

10   Robert Waldinger, What makes a good life? Lessons from the longest study on happiness, *TED.com* [video] (2016). Available at: www.ted.com/ talks/robert_waldinger_what_makes_a_good_life_lessons_from_the_longest_ study_on_happiness/transcript?language=en.

11   Quoted in Sarah Knapton, Five things you can do to be happier right now, *The Telegraph* (31 May 2015). Available at: www.telegraph.co.uk/culture/ hay-festival/11640753/Five-things-you-can-do-to-be-happier-right-now.html.

Is teaching the source of your stress?

It may be worth considering the other major causes of worry before assuming that teaching is the only issue that needs your attention.

The top sources of worry are money; health/fitness/weight; relationships with significant adults; your children; and too many social commitments/responsibilities.

If any of the above issues are impacting on your life, they should be tackled before or alongside exploration of your career options. Does teaching distress outrank the others listed? Does it cause, or exacerbate, the others?

Advice from teachers

I over-committed myself at work. I never said no and was taken in. A friend the same age as me was diagnosed with a terminal illness. The last time I saw her, she really told me off. She made me promise I'd say no. I did, and it has changed my life. I'd beg all the teachers working too hard to stop. Some say, how do you know if you're doing too much? I think, deep down, we all do know.

Georgia

Have you lost your passion for teaching?

Most people become teachers for noble reasons. They want to change the world (and why not? A few tweaks could be helpful). This can make it harder to admit it's not your calling after all. The old joke that primary teachers teach because they love children, secondary teachers teach because they love their subject and lecturers teach because they love themselves sheds light on where to redirect your passion. If you still love the idea of helping children, there are many options. If you retain a passion for your subject, there are options (see job list 5 (English) page 77, job list 6 (science) page 78 and jobs linked to degree subject pages 105–108). If you love yourself and think you have the answers, then start a blog, movement or tweet your ideas, and you'll quickly discover whether your peers concur.

> One of the symptoms of an approaching nervous breakdown is the belief that one's work is terribly important.
>
> Bertrand Russell, *The Conquest of Happiness*, p. 48

The elephant in the room?

The public sector is currently under enormous strain. Staff working in education, health and social care, prisons, the police and local government are being stretched and challenged like never before. It is admirable that so many people plough on despite the corrosive impact of budget cuts and increasing demands on services. However, it is not unreasonable to suggest that some individuals may want, or need, the opportunity to leave, temporarily or permanently, and pursue alternatives to regain mental and physical stability. I know that some people believe all staff should stay and fight until public services are properly respected and funded, but this can put even more pressure on decent individuals struggling on a personal level to do their best. It may take an even more severe recruitment and retention crisis to jolt politicians into the much needed paradigm shift; recognising and rewarding public sector workers for their dedication and positive impact rather than demonising and belittling their contribution to society. Assuming this shift isn't going to happen imminently, what can you do to safeguard your own job satisfaction and wellbeing in the meantime?

What do you feel immediately after the following thought experiment?

Try this thought experiment. Add five years to your current age and imagine you are in the same job as you are today.

Next, add ten years to your current age and think about what you have to do to be at the right-hand end of the scale.

Location, location, location

Perhaps the easiest problems to solve are those directly linked to specific people or places. A clash of personalities (colleagues or students) can be a major source of unhappiness at work. If it's genuinely short-term (a Year 13 pupil's overbearing parent or a head teacher leaving at the end of term), then you could mark off each day in one corner of your whiteboard and sit it out. If it's longer term, you could consider a change of employer rather than a change of career (see job list 1 pages 71–72). Moving sideways before burning your bridges completely can clarify the underlying reasons for your dissatisfaction, help you build a more impressive CV and expand your contacts and even horizons.

In my experience, people often focus all their frustrations and negativity on one person, place or even government. This is fine for short-term protection but ultimately it is only a delaying tactic. Life can't be put on hold indefinitely, as death has a habit of usurping procrastinators. Is your dissatisfaction really being caused by one demon (SLT, Ofsted, a parent, a pupil, lost car-parking space, a politician, the removal of chips from the canteen menu), or is it deeper? If it is deeper, check out where you are on your hero's journey (see page 41).

A teacher recently showed me a handwritten list he had made of all the people who are destroying education today. It was quite a list. I was relieved that careers advisers weren't on the list, but I was nervous in case he added me during our interview if my advice proved inadequate.

Surround yourself with positive teachers

Seek out the teachers in your school or broader network who are coping well, and ask for their secrets and tips. Successful people are always the most likely to share their methods. They're easy to spot – they're the ones smiling and moving!

The growing number of teaching networks online and in the form of regional groups such as Pedagoo.org and TeachMeets reduces the debilitating risk of professional isolation. Learning from other people's ideas and practice can be liberating.

The greener grass of better prospects elsewhere

Let's be clear: 'better prospects' can mean pay, challenge, personal development (career, social, family) or location. Have you been in your current role too long? There can be many altruistic reasons to stay put (loyalty to school/catchment area, to allow a partner's career to flourish, because your own children are settled, attachment to your colleagues/students). Eventually these may not be enough. If you do decide to stay put after you have identified good reasons for doing so, you can at least be reassured that you have a plan and you are implementing it. You can then explore ways to develop within more constricted boundaries. For example, you could develop new hobbies, qualifications, interests or research interests that allow you to grow. The general rule is to stay long enough in a role to stretch yourself and develop new skills/knowledge, but not long enough to stagnate. Easier said than done, I know, but three years is usually enough time in a role, unless there are natural changes, and three years is a long time in teaching, with plenty of change naturally occurring. Do check out all options for genuine growth (not just taking on extra work that doesn't help you grow) within your current department and school before applying for other positions. Talk to a trusted colleague.

The grass may not be greener on the other side. Teachers across the world face similar challenges. Can you guess which country these authors are describing?

> We're counting on our teachers to shape and transform our next generation, but we pay them salaries comparable to that of someone who works at a rental car counter. We expect them to deal with learning, family, motivational, and life issues for hundreds of students yet decide that they are so untrustworthy that we need to hold their feet to the fire with nonsensical standardized tests. We blame them when things don't go exactly the way we want ... yet we do next to nothing to support

them. Yet they persevere, and come to school every day committed to helping our kids become better people.

Tony Wagner and Ted Dintersmith, *Most Likely to Succeed*

It is the US education system, but they could be talking about virtually any country across the globe.

Advice from teachers

Don't keep waiting for the dream job vacancy at your current school. It may never come or may be given to someone else when it does.

Paul

Surviving the rest of the week

Here are some tips to help you cope in the short term, to get through the exhausting daily grind. Write down all the things you have to do and rank them. In brackets, write the date each has to be completed by. Is it possible to do everything on time? If yes, take a deep breath and get started. If no, identify things you are going to delegate or not complete. If you're not going to complete something, let people involved know so they can make other arrangements.

- If someone is not happy, show them your to-do list.
- Say no to extra work.
- Make some 'me' time.
- Have a positive attitude – don't be a victim, hero or villain.
- Talk to someone you trust for some support.
- Avoid staffroom politics/gossip.

> Whatever you can do, or dream you can, begin it; boldness has genius, power and magic in it.
>
> John Anster (inspired by Goethe, Faust)

Some food for thought

Complete the following sentences without thinking for too long, and then review your responses.

If I knew I couldn't fail, I would …

....

When I'm at my best, I am [add adjectives here].

....

If I could change anything about myself, it would be …

....

My top skills are …

....

In five years' time I'd like to …

....

What I need to do to get there is …

....

These are the people who can help me the most …

....

I'm at my happiest when …

....

What's missing is …

....

Common career mistakes made by teachers who feel stuck

Teachers who are dedicated to their students but who neglect themselves can be left behind. It seems unfair, but it's no accident. Here's why this happens.

- Not blowing your own trumpet. If nobody knows you're good, then opportunities are likely to pass you by.

- Waiting to look for new opportunities until it's too late. Looking to move on when you're coasting or struggling can look desperate. It's best to start looking while things are going well.

- Not looking for opportunities in the right places. We need to be proactive; flicking through the *TES* vacancy section once a year is not enough. See pages 65–66 and 104 for the full range of sources.

- Not looking regularly enough. Busy people can still make time to look after their own career. Dedicate at least an hour per week. Try the checklist on pages 8–9 to help you identify which tactics will help you use your time most efficiently.

- Ignoring the approaches used by successful people around you. What are the people who are doing well doing that you're not?

- Giving up too soon. Your career is a long-term and ongoing commitment! Don't give up after a few months. Developing your teaching craft can take a few years. There have never been more books and blogs available to help you with your subject, behaviour management or any aspect of teaching that seems beyond your current comfort zone.

- Having unrealistic or narrow targets. Keep an open mind, because there are so many opportunities available and some you can create all for yourself.

- Doing it all on your own. Build a network of people who know your strengths and aims – you'll be amazed at how helpful they can be. Help others to achieve their goals; when they move on, they may be able to help you.

The ghosts of fear

Napoleon Hill, in *Think and Grow Rich*, describes six deep-seated fears that can sabotage our progress.[12] They are poverty (or a significant loss of income), criticism, ill-health, old age, death and losing the love of someone. All of these fears can be overcome. These fears are welded to procrastination as strongly as Ant is to Dec. And none of these is worth being miserable for the final thirty years of your life. Whether you have more or fewer years remaining is irrelevant. The only fear we should really have is wasting our life. Blink and it's gone!

Write down what specifically bothers you about each of these fears. Rephrase, if necessary, so each item is stated as a positive action you can take to negate the fear. What is the positive intent behind the fear? What are you really protecting yourself from?

Concentrate on taking action on these.

For example:

Loss of income

A loss of income can deter many teachers from moving on. Have a good look at the short- and long-term impact of a change. Is security with misery really worth it?

---

12 Napoleon Hill, *Think and Grow Rich* (Chichester: Capstone, 2009 [1937]).

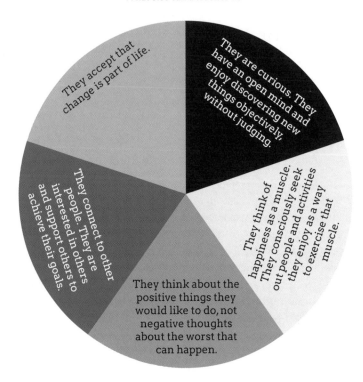

They are curious. They have an open mind and enjoy discovering new things objectively, without judging.

They accept that change is part of life.

They connect to other people. They are interested in others and support others to achieve their goals.

They think about the positive things they would like to do, not negative thoughts about the worst that can happen.

They think of happiness as a muscle. They consciously seek out people and activities they enjoy as a way to exercise that muscle.

Five things happy people do

All the world's a stage

Are you a hero, victim or villain?

We often get trapped in a psychological bind at work – or, worse, in life.

If we convince ourselves we are one of the following three characters, we are doomed to unhappiness. Check you do not identify with any of these. If you do see yourself playing one of these roles, follow the advice on how to extricate yourself before it is too late.

Hero/rescuer

Are you the hero in your job? Are you saving others from dis-aster? Are you controlling? Do you have a compelling cause that drives you? Do you give more than you receive? Is your catchphrase or mantra 'I must keep on going, as only I can save the day'?

Victim

Do you feel picked on or put upon? Powerless? Overwhelmed? Do you just take on extra work, burdened like a donkey or ass? Do you suffer in silence as the slings and arrows fire at you? Is your catchphrase 'No, I'll do it, because if it wasn't for me the whole place would fall into ruin'? A stereotypical teenager believing life is so unfair can be embroiled in this role, with 'headless chicken' anger thrown into the mix.

Villain

Have you become so disillusioned or jaded that you snipe from the sidelines, tweeting negatively to belittle the heroes and vic-tims who are your colleagues or children you are supposed to be inspiring? Do you think in terms of 'them' and 'they' rather than 'we' and 'us'?

If you are in any of the above places psychologically (you may even flip between all three), you must rethink your thinking. We are not characters in a Hollywood B movie. We are adults, but as emotional rather than rational creatures we easily slip into these three roles. We must step back from falling into these dangerous mindsets in case we become stuck there per-manently. We must realise that we can be in control of our own lives. If we do not take control of our own lives, we are letting someone else (head teacher, politicians, pupils, etc.) be in charge of us. Many teachers have found the above framework useful as a way to make sense of their current position. Anything that helps us dissociate from a 'stuck' place can be liberating.

Living in the moment

Insights from religion, philosophy, psychology and history suggest that happiness and fulfilment are at their peak for those of us who are able to live in the moment – but not *for* the moment – not in the ugly solipsistic or hedonistic way some Western new age movements have misinterpreted Buddhist and Taoist traditions, where exploring and finding yourself excludes connections with others (people and place) rather than strengthening them. Being present while appreciating the bigger trajectory of our lives is what leads to ultimate satisfaction and pleasure.

> The more one studies attempted solutions to problems in politics and economics, in art, philosophy and religion, the more one has the impression of extremely gifted people wearing out their ingenuity at the impossible and futile task of trying to get the water of life into neat and permanent packages ... If happiness always depends on something expected in the future, we are chasing a will-o'-the-wisp that ever eludes our grasp, until the future, and ourselves, vanish into the abyss of death.
>
> Alan Watts, *The Wisdom of Insecurity,* pp. 14–15

The insight can both help and hinder your decision-making process. When we're stuck in an unpleasant present, rather than living fully within it, we can feel overwhelmed and less able to make good decisions; we need distance to connect us to our long-term trajectory and its reassuring perspective. The case studies of teachers changing direction reveal this truth.

Advice from teachers

I studied English and history of art at university, and planned to follow a career in museum or gallery work. After completing a postgraduate qualification in museum and galleries studies, it was difficult to find paid employment so I taught English abroad and worked in theatre administration. However, I was always interested in working in education, so I did a Postgraduate Certificate of Education (PGCE) and became an English teacher. While I enjoyed aspects of teaching, such as lesson planning, thinking of creative ways to deliver my subject and being with young people, I became disillusioned by the lack of support from the school. I left to take up an exciting new post at Cambridge University, where I developed the university's Widening Participation programme. It was great to work with academics and undergraduates in developing new projects designed to motivate and inspire youngsters. From there I moved to Lambeth Education Authority, where I worked on the Aimhigher and Gifted and Talented programmes. I particularly enjoyed exploring the theory of how and why we learn and applying it in ways to support students, especially focusing on the more able. I had a break to bring up my young children as my husband's job took us to Brussels for a few years, and then returned to teaching English. I taught in a bilingual school where I had the freedom to teach keen students without the pressure of exams at the end of the year. I felt I now had the right mix of skills, confidence and experience to be at my best as a teacher, which I lacked in my first teaching job. I now work at Warwick University teaching on the PGCE course and working on projects to raise student aspiration. While I have never consciously planned my career, I have always been in roles that have teaching and learning at their core. Maybe you want to call it luck, but I've always been open to new opportunities that have taken my career beyond the classroom and I have been especially lucky in having mentors who

recognised the range of skills I could offer and who supported me.

Rosemary

Most of the teachers I have interviewed for this book have had
a career path that is neither smooth nor dazzling. They move
jobs a few times, sometimes sideways and backwards, and do
not progress in a linear way.

The main point here is to keep on moving.

A hero's journey

Joseph Campbell came up with the intriguing idea that all our lives follow the same basic trajectory. This pattern, the monomyth, is portrayed in most films, novels and TV dramas.[13] It is rumoured that George Lucas and the *Star Wars* writers studied this format and used it as a template for the ubiquitous franchise.

Where are you on your journey?

Pondering this question can reveal important clues relating to your next steps.

1 **Call to arms and refusal.** We are living in an ordinary world. An experience or event makes us wonder if there is more than this current mundane reality. We first realise we are part of the world and could make an impact. We are told, or feel, we are special, and must go on a journey to fulfil our potential. We initially refuse the call because we doubt ourselves. This lack of self-belief or confidence is a narrative driving so many lives. I meet many people in their thirties and forties who have told me they have not really started living their real life yet. Wow. If you feel you're at this point in your journey, you need to build your self-belief before moving on to the next step, to avoid making fragile or false steps. Retraining is often the way people build confidence to prepare for big changes later. Moving in one go is often too much for people who lack confidence. See pages 10–15 for ways to build your confidence.

2 **Crossing the threshold.** Eventually we do rise to the challenge and cross the threshold into a new, alien world. In films this can literally be a new world. For us, this can

---

13 See Joseph Campbell, *The Hero with a Thousand Faces*, Bollingen Series XVII, third edition (Novato, CA: New World Library, 2008).

be leaving home to go to university or start a job. We face challenges and serve an apprenticeship, usually assisted by a mentor or guide. We think we're learning external skills but we're really building internal strengths, such as values and resilience, to help us succeed in the long term. The challenges could be difficult teacher training placements or our first awful job, supervisor or class. We must overcome genuine difficulties and slay a dragon or two. Many teachers find themselves in this place – struggling, but wondering if there is light at the end of the tunnel. Asking themselves: will it suddenly click into place or will the gruelling cycle of preparation, delivery, marking and assessment be my groundhog day? Your mentor can help you clarify your position. In the middle of it, you may find objectivity difficult, so a holiday or chat with trusted colleagues can be invaluable.

> **TIP** Visit a favourite place to contemplate your future, as you'll be relaxed and more confident out of your usual environment. Also, being away from your routine will give you perspective.

The challenge can be to discover whether there is a niche within teaching to suit you, or whether a more radical step is your answer. Ultimately, we conquer, find wisdom, humility and are 'masters'. We have added all the best human qualities to balance our self-belief and confidence. Some realise that teaching is not the right path, but was merely an important step along life's journey. It can be difficult to admit this to yourself or others, but it's worth it. On their deathbeds, people regret time they wasted rather than mistakes they made.

3   **The return.** We return to the real world to share our riches and pass on our wisdom to the next generation. This could be applying our new knowledge in the classroom, building a successful department or starting a new career

or business. If you don't feel you're at this point in your journey, then go back to steps 1 and 2 and work out where you are. You can repeat this sequence of steps more than once, though probably not as many times as Luke Skywalker, who appears to be caught in a *Groundhog Day* version of the hero's journey as part of a never-ending series of *Star Wars* films!

The layers of an onion

Are you a teacher by identity, personality, job title, interest or environment?

The logical levels model developed by Robert Dilts can be a useful aid to career decision-making.[14] In it, like a Russian doll, we are made up of different layers.

Identity

At our core is our identity. This is our authentic self – linked to our life's purpose – and it is fundamental that we live our life in accord within our sense of identity. This is the 'why?' of our life. Some people are teachers at the identity level; it is who they were, are and will be. It is part of their DNA and they could not lead a fulfilling life without living this role. These people tend to remain teachers for the long haul. The advantage to the education system, or the other workplaces where they're often found, such as the NHS and RSPCA, is that they retain a dedicated, committed worker who will often put the needs and welfare of their students, patients or animals before their own without blinking. It's also why they get more upset

---

14   See Robert Dilts, *Changing Belief Systems with NLP* (Capitola, CA: Meta Publications, 1990), p. 1.

about people eroding their capacity to do their job well than being paid less than they deserve. This dedication and 'beyond the call of duty' philosophy can also hurt these individuals, as they are prone to suffer stress-related illness in the long term and must ensure they take care of themselves and their own families as well as they care for those they serve at work. They can change career, but it has to match their sense of identity.

In his blog 'Curmudgucation', teacher Peter Greene eloquently sums up the thoughts and implications of an identity-level teacher, writing a letter to his Board of Education. His letter is worth a read.[15] Tip: If you spot a teacher becoming really agitated and purple from the neck upwards when an educational outsider pontificates about teaching it is a sure sign they are experiencing an attack of their identity. This triggers a fight, fright, flight response. This is identity theft at its most pernicious.

Personality/Skill

This is the 'what' we do and 'how' we do it. These teachers teach because they have a natural or learned flair and skill across the skill set essential for great teaching. They enjoy their work because they are good at it. They could easily move on to other jobs that require the same skill set.

Those teaching at the interest level are focused on their subject. This is more likely to apply to teachers working in specialist roles such as a canoe instructor, a teacher of the deaf, an art teacher or fitness instructor. Changing careers to other roles based around their interest is the logical step if teaching has lost its pull.

---

15 See Peter Greene, A not quitting letter, *Curmudgucation* [blog] (4 November 2015). Available at: http://curmudgucation.blogspot.co.uk/2015/11/a-not-quitting-letter.html.

Environment

This is the 'where' – our place of work. Few teachers are primarily driven by an environment focus. This would include people working because the place is convenient, perhaps near to a dependent elderly relative or other commitments linked to a geographical area. In the past this had a bigger influence on career choice, before commuting and relocation became an expectation. Career change is not just linked to the content of the work, which can be good or bad. Environment can also be important as a factor in a negative context, pushing people away – for example, the school or classroom could be crumbling around you. A change of environment could reinvigorate your work.

In the next section we will explore these three levels.

Who are you?

The following list of thirty-two identity words should help you clarify your true identity:

teacher, warrior, communicator, guide, instructor, parent, sage, adviser, helper, magician, comedian, organiser, trainer, creator, counsellor, inventor, entrepreneur, leader, manager, strategist, mentor, catalyst, healer, writer, advocate, protector, inspector, supervisor, carer, performer, explorer, improviser

Circle the words that most appeal to you.

Reflect on how you can apply these in your work.

If you're unsure, look through some of the job ideas in Part 3 of this book. The key identity words are listed with each job.

We think of ourselves in different ways. In *Shrek*, the ogre opens up to Donkey by explaining that he is like an onion. He feels judged by his outer layers (his aesthetically challenging appearance and angry demeanour). His struggle is in revealing his true identity to Fiona and Donkey to allow him to be his authentic self.

If you see yourself as a teacher at your core layer of identity you will wrestle uncomfortably with thoughts of leaving the profession, because it is a challenge to you, the person. If so, you need to reassess how you can redefine or balance your identity through alternative ways of working.

It's worth thinking about your identity, because it can explain how we can make bad choices and decisions. I wouldn't usually mention Nelson Mandela, Tony Blair and Margaret Thatcher in the same sentence, but they all shared a strong sense of identity and made decisions based on their inner belief. Sometimes evidence from the real world is ignored and decisions are made which can turn out well (ending apartheid and the rebirth of South Africa) – or not so well (the Iraq war, the poll tax). Teachers must be wary of this trap. If being a teacher is part of who you believe you are, then you could consider alternative jobs with teaching at their core. If it's creating a fairer society with opportunities for all, there are roles outside the classroom in which you can make a big impact.

Remember, you are more than your job, even if you feel passionately melded to it.

Psychologist Martin Seligman has identified six signature strengths.[16] We express our identity by living through one of more of these.

---

16 See Martin E. P. Seligman, *Authentic Happiness: Using the New Positive Psychology to Realize Your Potential for Lasting Fulfillment* (New York: Free Press, 2002).

Which of these six appeal to you?

(curiosity, love of learning, judgement, ingenuity, emotional intelligence, perspective)

(valour, perseverance, integrity)

WISDOM

COURAGE

(kindness, loving)

(citizenship, fairness, leadership)

HUMANITY

JUSTICE

TEMPERANCE

(self-control, prudence, humility)

TRANSCENDENCE

(gratitude, hope, spirituality, forgiveness, humour, zest, aestheticism)

If you are a teacher at the level of personality you can far more easily identify alternative careers that will showcase your personality, strengths and skills.

It's quite rare to meet teachers who think of teaching as just a job: a convenient way to fill their day or fit in with personal circumstances. They avoid the swirling vortex of angst associated with a career change for those for whom teaching is more than a job.

Starting to look elsewhere for a job

First, let's start with some good news. These are the top skills required by graduate employers according to targetjobs.co.uk:

- good communication
- being able to convey ideas and listen to others, negotiate and persuade
- effective leadership and management
- directing and motivating others to achieve goals, delegating, planning and coordinating skills
- planning and research skills: the ability to create a plan to accomplish specified objectives
- the ability to collect, analyse and interpret information
- teamwork[17]

As a teacher you will have demonstrated all seven of these skills on a daily basis. So the world is your oyster, sort of. The small print includes a few restrictions; terms and conditions that we'll explore in the pages ahead. But the overall vibe is positive. Do not sit like that member of staff slumped in his staffroom chair with a slightly haunted look in his eyes, as if he's seen into his future and is both terrified by and resigned to his fate. There are options. Which of these words appeal to you? These can be the building blocks of a satisfying career. They are split between 'personal' and 'specialist' skills. These are the words that appear most commonly on job descriptions and person specifications.

> Personal: imaginative, delegator, dynamic, energetic, presenter, communicator, empathetic, motivator, sensitive, flexible, methodical, persistent, inquisitive, tactful, co-ordinator, assertive, friendly, tolerant, adaptable, balanced, realistic, practical, proactive, driven, tenacious, positive, honest, versatile, loyal, punctual.

> Specialist: foreign-language speaker, telephone skills, cultural awareness, creative, problem-solver, IT/computer software user, budgeting, sales, business acumen.

---

17 See https://targetjobs.co.uk/careers-advice/career-planning/273051-the-top-10-skills-thatll-get-you-a-job-when-you-graduate.

A solution to writer's – and teacher's – block?

Raymond Chandler once said, on making a book more exciting: 'When in doubt, have a man come through a door with a gun in his hand.' Chandler may not have meant this to apply to non-fiction, but let's give it a go. Please play along. If a sinister man suddenly entered the room now, pressed a cold gun to your temple, and asked you if you really wanted to be a teacher for the next ten years, what would your answer be? Your life depends upon answering the question honestly. If you're thinking 'no' or 'don't think so' then read on. If you're thinking 'yes', you can stop here and find another book to browse, or continue this one voyeuristically just to make sure. If this activity is a little too grisly, be aware that it is based on a technique to overcome procrastination, which is a major cause of career and life dissatisfaction.

Advice from teachers

My first move was through choice, my second through 'restructuring'.

I loved being a classroom teacher. During my time as a main-scale primary teacher, I taught across all year groups and held coordinator posts for music and ICT. Gradually, the freedom I had in teaching, and what I knew was right in terms of curriculum delivery, was being eroded by more and more government initiatives. I was looking for a way out of the classroom and an opportunity to continue teaching in an area of interest to me. I found a position in the local authority as an ICT advisory teacher, which led to my managing three City Learning Centres in the borough. I had the freedom to influence the use of technology in schools and implement a number of exciting initiatives, including leading on an Apple Regional Training Centre and LEGO Education Centre. I also developed a relationship with Nintendo UK, and introduced many schools in the borough to games-based learning.

In 2011, I was made redundant due to government cuts and faced a difficult decision. Did I go back into the classroom or go it alone? I chose the latter, and with a partner set up a consultancy offering computing support to schools. This turned out to be the best decision. I now work with many schools from across the country. Being freelance has enabled me to help schools (through staff INSET and working with students) implement creative ways of using technology in their curriculums and the delivery of the statutory requirements. I also work with larger companies and consultancies, such as Apple and LEGO Education, training teachers in the UK and beyond.

I am still involved in education, and still consider myself a teacher. This time, though, it's on my own terms. Being made redundant was, ironically, the best thing that could have happened to me. I am still passionate about education and feel that I am making a difference in a way that I couldn't if I was still in the classroom.

Stuart

What kind of company do you want to work for?

You can narrow down your search by considering the type and size of employer you'd like to work for. This section can also help you select the key drivers underpinning your ideal type of employer. Furthermore, it demonstrates that no job choice is perfect; all have advantages and disadvantages.

Which of these environments appeal?

Multinational company

+ structured training, progression and social networks

+ higher salary and security

– less freedom to develop at your own pace

– less variety of job tasks

Public sector (health/ social service, LAs)

+ responsibility and positive impact

+ structured training and progression

– lower salary

– challenging and difficult environments

Voluntary/ non-profit-making

+ your work aligned with your values/beliefs

+ challenge and impact

– insecurity/short-term contracts

– lower salary

SMEs (service sector/industry/ manufacturing) franchisee

+ variety and challenge

+ early responsibility and own initiative

– insecurity/vulnerable to economic cycles

– fewer formal training and progression routes

None of the above/ self-employment/ freelance

+ responsibility and control

+ variety

– insecurity of income

– isolation and long hours (but flexible)

Using your personality as a guide to alternative career ideas

Consider the following as a way to uncover your primary career drivers and to generate ideas for a new career. Choose your preferences: A or B and 1 or 2, which will correspond to the following lists A1, A2, B1 and B2. Thinking about work …

(A) I prefer to know what I'm supposed to be doing, what the tasks are, the steps and processes involved, and what I'm expected to understand and expedite.

OR

(B) I prefer to use my imagination, ingenuity and creativity to make a contribution to a workplace.

Plus:

(1) I prefer to work with people at the core of my work, either helping them directly to improve their current position or indirectly by providing a service.

OR

(2) I prefer to focus on tasks, understanding and applying practical procedures or analysing complex ideas or theories.

The lists that follow give examples of different types of job which fit with these preferences. Read them and see if any appeal to you.

A1: Practical services and support to people

Air cabin crew

Careers adviser

Estate agent

Funeral director

Health promotion specialist

Hypnotherapist

Insurance claims handler

Legal executive

Recruitment consultant

Solicitor

Tour guide

Visitor attraction manager

Volunteer organiser

A2: Practical problem-solver: business/skill focus

Accommodation manager

Accountant/auditor/
technician

Air traffic controller

Conference/exhibition
organiser

Court support worker

Driving instructor

Librarian

Marketing executive

Ofsted inspector

Police officer

Prison officer

Scene of crime officer

B1: Creative and personal development/support

Actor

Complementary and alternative medicine practitioner

Clown

Journalist

Marketing executive

Nurse

Paramedic

Psychologist (educational/child)

Public relations officer

Solicitor

Speech and language therapist

Voiceover artist

Writer (education)

Youth worker

B2: Creative and technical problem-solving

Accommodation manager

Chocolate taster

Conference/exhibition organiser

Crossword compiler

Inventor

Lab technician

NHS clinical scientist

Probation officer

Programmer

Scene of crime officer

Stand-up comedian

Solicitor

What motivates you to go to work?

The most common responses to the question, 'What motivates you to go to work?' are as follows.

Money for treats

To be able to hop on the hedonistic treadmill and be a purchaser in our consumption-driven society: to buy holidays, clothes, shoes, football season tickets, National Trust membership, cinema tickets, books, cars, vinyl records, fast or fancy food …

Money for essentials

To pay the mortgage/rent, utility bills, insurance and avoid poverty. Some people include things from the 'treats' list here. I'm not judging, just aiming for accuracy.

Social contact

To meet colleagues and
friends at work and
share conversations and
experiences.

To contribute something useful/meaningful

To society generally or to specific people
or projects that are of interest to you. If
this is lacking, then the work inevitably
becomes boring and unsatisfying, and
people will only stay if they feel they
have no alternatives.

These motivators reveal that much of our work satisfaction is derived from the social contacts we make at work. This usually involves being around people who are similar to us. Teachers often report feeling isolated from other adults for most of their working day. Bear in mind these three key components of a satisfying job (money left after living costs, social contact and meaning) when considering alternative careers, as these factors can be as important as job tasks, location and salary package.

Now fill in your own list using the same four headings. If you include all your bills, direct debits and estimate how much money you spend per week, you can work out what salary you need for the lifestyle you seek. Most people do it the other way around.

The magic salary for optimum happiness is around £50,000 per annum, according to research by economist Angus Deaton and psychologist Daniel Kahneman from Princeton University.[18] Since most people working in the UK earn less than this figure, the impact of social contact and meaning become more important. Most teachers are not primarily motivated by money, but many people are. The individuals at the top of companies and organisations are usually motivated by money. They then think paying people more – for example, to train as a teacher in a subject in which there is a shortage of teachers – will improve teaching standards. It will not. I've asked groups of teachers, 'How many of you would give yourself a bonus worth one year's salary if the money had to come from the school budget and cuts would need to be made to fund it?' Not one teacher said they'd take it.

Politicians and bankers are different to teachers. That's why they shouldn't run public services.

---

18   Belinda Luscombe, Do we need $75,000 a year to be happy? *Time* (6 September 2010). Available at: http://content.time.com/time/magazine/article/0,9171,2019628,00.html.

What motivates you to go to work?

Treats per month/year

....
....
....
....

Essentials per month/year

....
....
....
....

Social contact

....
....
....
....

To add meaning

....
....
....
....

Skills list

All jobs require a mix of general or transferable skills and specialist skills. A dog groomer and an air traffic controller have specialist skills related to the equipment they operate, as well as personal skills such as concentration and attention to detail.

General/transferable skills fit into ten categories.

1. Communication

Communicating effectively in words, talking to people, explaining ideas and needs. Many people find the idea of presenting ideas to groups abhorrent. Teachers who are comfortable and confident speaking to groups have an edge at interviews and in most jobs where presentation skills are routinely required.

2. Reflection

Thinking about your work and contribution, and the long-term direction of the company.

3. Logical

Understanding the facts and detail, following instructions, setting goals, enacting procedures, following all steps involved to complete tasks.

4. Creativity

Being creative and imaginative, spotting opportunities, thinking laterally, having a vision.

5. People

Understanding people, helpful, reading their feelings and emotions, empathetic, able to lead, supervise and motivate teams and individuals and handle complaints.

6. Task focus

Good at making objective decisions and giving and receiving feedback.

7. Organisation

Organised, finishes tasks, able to prioritise, good at keeping accurate records and time management.

8. Flexible

Learning quickly, adaptability, good at trouble-shooting.

9. Positivity

Having a positive outlook, creating and spreading a 'can do' atmosphere.

10. Awareness

Awareness of danger – stress, faults, errors, system breakdowns, competition, threats facing an organisation.

Advice from teachers

I was pondering self-employment. I asked the window cleaner I use about his transition to self-employment. He put me in contact with his accountant. I had a free chat with her and received some great advice. It helped me feel I was moving rather than being stuck.

Helen

Who could I speak to about changing job?

You could start a list of jobs you are considering. Start with any ideas you had before reading this book, and then add any additional ideas you find in the job lists and descriptions.

Do you know anyone doing the job?

Do you know someone working in a company employing people in the role?

If so, ask if you can speak to them about their job. Write down all the questions you would like answers to, but don't interrogate the person! Keep the vibe light and 'chat-show' style. Start by asking them about their own career path. Most people's favourite topic of conversation is their own life, so this is usually a good place to start. Find out about the job market, especially locally, if that is important to you. Ask for further leads.

You could find other contacts using the following resources:

Recruitment agencies specialising in the sector you are considering.

....

....

....

....

....

Local press/the internet for companies that are expanding in your area. Contacting companies before jobs are advertised can give you an edge.

....

....

....

....

....

Specialist communities via journals, trade magazines, Twitter groups, web forums, conferences and exhibitions, and national training organisations (NTOs).

....

....

....

....

....

Employer events such as company open days, visits and work-shadowing opportunities. These can be nurtured while you are still in teaching by arranging visits for your students and going along with them. Do take some students with a genuine interest in the company, though, or you may be rumbled.

....

....

....

....

....

Volunteering can give you an insight into a specific company or job role. It may seem a time-consuming option, but changing career is a bigger commitment, so this can be a vital insight confirming or ending your interest in a specific option. If your proposed career change involves freelance work, then submit speculative ideas of your own.

....

....

....

....

....

Training – are there any training courses or events available that would build your experience and contacts? For example, yoga, skiing, wine-tasting, meditation day or weekend courses are available. Check the Workers' Educational Association (WEA), Open University and local further education (FE) college course directories for ideas.

....

....

....

....

....

It is useful to continuously engage in the above networking activities, not just when you're looking for a new direction. It is estimated that only 20–30% of all jobs are advertised.[19] The bulk of the job market is hidden, and networking helps us see this broader range of opportunities. It also helps to lead us to the niche employers and jobs that best fit our skills and values.

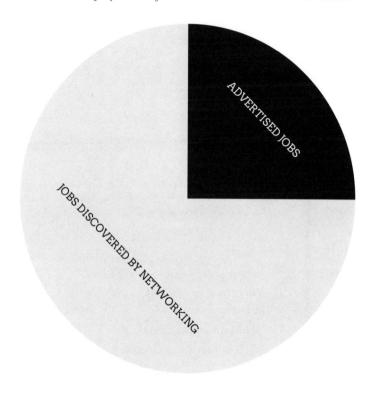

---

19 Peter Hawkins, *The Art of Building Windmills: Career Tactics for the 21st Century* (Liverpool: Graduate Into Employment Unit, University of Liverpool, 1999).

Jobs and salaries

£130k .... Broker £130,000

£120k

£110k .... Chief executive £110,000

£100k

£90k .... Aircraft pilot £90,000

Marketing/sales director £83,000
£80k .... IT director £80,000
Advertising/PR director £78,000

Air traffic controller £75,000

Legal professional £73,000
£70k .... Medical practitioner £69,000

Actuary, economist, statistician £62,000
£60k .... Senior police officer £59,000

HR manager £56,000

Sales (accounts/business manager) £52,000
£50k .... Senior officer in fire/ambulance service £48,000 ⟵
Solicitor £47,000

Insurance underwriter £43,000 ⟵
£40k .... Quantity surveyor £41,000

Jobs with salaries lower than teachers

Nurse £26,000
Musician £22,000
Forest worker £21,000
Youth and community worker £20,500
Bar manager £18,500
Farm worker £18,000
Chef £17,500
Travel agent £17,000
Window cleaner £15,000
Florist £10,000
Bar staff £8,000

IT project manager £48,000   Health service manager £48,000

Architect £43,000   Management consultant £44,000

The anatomy of a job

Qualifications

Will you need further qualifications? If a job advert says they are essential, then yes you do.

If desirable or preferable, then ask first. You could save a lot of time and money.

Skills and experience

Do you have enough?

Are your skills relevant and transferable?

If you need more, identify how you can acquire these.

Workplace

Where will you be working?

What are the main tasks?

What does a typical day look like?

Pay

Don't just look at the salary. Factor in living expenses and travel to work.

Are there other benefits? Health cover, pension, perks, allowances?

With whom?

Who will you be around most of the time? Your line manager, colleagues, clients?

Themed job lists

Here are some lists of jobs to generate thought.

Make a note of any that appeal, and take a look at the more detailed information in Part 3 (page 119).

JOB LIST 1

Teaching

For many qualified teachers, moving sideways into a different teaching role can be a perfect next step. It helps many to find their true niche within the huge swathe of educational careers. It helps others on their way out of teaching in a dignified and considered manner. The case studies in this section highlight the powerful impact a small change can make, either as a metaphorical pause for breath or as a satisfying destination.

As mentioned earlier, unless you are certain about your next step, then making the smallest change possible is wise. Changes within school, between schools, age group, subject, country, and teaching support roles are all worth considering.

- Dance/music/drama teacher
- Driving instructor
- Early Years teacher
- Education officer (museum, public/private body)
- Education technician
- EFL (English as a foreign language) teacher

- Fitness instructor
- Further education (FE) lecturer/tutor
- Higher education (HE) lecturer
- Learning mentor
- National Vocational Qualifications (NVQ) assessor
- Online tutor
- Open University (OU) lecturer
- Outdoor activities instructor
- Play worker
- Primary teacher
- Private tutor
- Secondary teacher
- Special educational needs (SEN) teacher
- Supply teacher
- Teacher (film set, travellers)
- Teacher (pupil referral unit)
- Training officer
- Youth and community worker

Moving away from teaching

Social support

If you're considering a tentative move away from teaching, then providing personal and social support to individuals or groups is a logical next step. The difference between working with groups and individuals is massive. People, especially teenagers, act very differently in groups and one-to-one. As a careers adviser sitting in the staffroom, I would have a list of the Year 11s I'd be interviewing that day. Invariably a teacher would glance down the list and pick out one name and suck in air through their teeth and warn me that a particular lad would be trouble. Without fail, he would be charming and polite. Often I would be the first adult who had sat down with him and really listened to him, asking what he wanted to do before stepping in with information, advice or guidance.

Levels of support

Although these overlap, and definitions can be flexible, it is useful to explore the different roles available to identify the areas in which you are most interested.

Information: providing information about choices without offering your interpretation or opinion, often working on telephone helplines or remotely, using technology.

Coaching: helping others develop, learn new skills, define and achieve personal success, and meet challenges.

Advice: offering an opinion or recommendation based on an assessment of someone's situation or needs.

Guidance: advice provided at a professional level that has a significant impact on the recipient.

Counselling: the process of guiding someone through change using specialist skills and knowledge, usually over a longer period of time.

Talking therapy: an intervention (talking and/or treatment) to remedy, alleviate, rehabilitate or cure a disorder.

JOB LIST 2

- Accommodation manager
- Advocate
- British Sign Language worker
- Care assistant
- Careers adviser
- Community education/development coordinator
- Counsellor
- Drama/art/music therapist
- Education welfare officer (EWO)
- Educational/child psychologist
- Foster carer
- Hypnotherapist
- Local authority (LA) school support
- Life coach
- MP/trade union official
- Prison officer
- Probation officer
- Psychologist
- Sign language interpreter
- Social worker
- Volunteer organiser
- Youth offending team worker

JOB LIST 3

Roles in health care

This offers a different, but overlapping, range of jobs compared to the preceding lists. All involve helping people directly, but in health service roles the proportion of therapeutic and science-based interventions is increased. If this suits your background or interests, then there are dozens of jobs to consider, including those listed below.

- Acupuncturist
- Alexander technique therapist
- Chiropractor
- Clinical scientist
- Cognitive behavioural therapist
- Dentist
- Dietitian
- Doctor
- Health promotion specialist
- Nurse
- Occupational therapist
- Operating department practitioner
- Osteopath
- Paramedic
- Podiatrist
- Speech and language therapist

JOB LIST 4

Working with other people (not in a caring role)

There are millions of jobs providing services to people. These require all levels of training, from professional through to training on the job. People and communication skills are the bedrock of most jobs, and surveys regularly show that meeting and serving the public is a hugely positive contributor to job satisfaction and variety. If you are drained or daunted by the burden of expectancy in roles where you are the named provider of help to vulnerable people, then this area of work could be a positive option.

- Accountant, auditor, technician
- Administrative role (court, estates officer, purchasing manager, registrar)
- Adventure travel guide
- Air cabin crew
- Beauty therapist
- Bingo caller
- Clown
- Comedian
- Conference organiser
- Dog handler
- Estate agent
- Funeral director
- Insurance claims handler
- Journalist
- Librarian
- Licensed conveyancer
- Marketing executive
- MP/trade union official
- Police officer
- Recruitment consultant
- Tour guide
- Visitor attraction manager

JOB LIST 5

English/working with words

If you'd like to build your work around words and communication, there are many roles worth considering. See below for a selection.

- Copy-editor
- Crossword compiler
- Educational writer
- Human resources officer
- Journalist
- Legal executive
- Librarian
- MP/trade union official
- PR executive
- Professional speaker
- Recruitment consultant
- Solicitor
- Speech and language therapist
- Tour guide
- Voiceover artist

JOB LIST 6

Science-related roles

Scientific knowledge and skills (analysis, attention to detail, creativity, strategy, exploration, inspection) form the basis of many careers. If these could be the core of your career satisfaction, then the following roles could be worth your consideration.

- Accountant
- Auditor
- NHS clinical scientist
- Surveyor
- Insurance claims handler
- Psychologist
- Air traffic controller
- Chocolate taster
- Inventor
- Lab technician
- Sales rep (science products)
- Scene of crime officer
- Health promotion specialist
- Journalist (science/technology)
- Visitor attraction guide (science)
- Complementary and alternative medicine practitioner
- Paramedic
- Clinical psychologist

JOB LIST 7

Performing roles

For teachers who thrive on the adrenalin rush of performing to groups, there are many positive alternatives. This part of teaching is often both the main reason cited for leaving the profession and the element most missed by some who leave! The list presented here provides some food for thought for those who would like to retain an element of the heady mix of performance, improvisation and spontaneity which is often difficult to recreate outside the classroom.

- Actor
- Adventure travel guide
- Art/drama/music therapist
- British Sign Language worker
- Circus performer
- Clown
- Conference/exhibition organiser
- Health promotion specialist
- Journalist
- Professional speaker
- Ski/snowboard instructor
- Stand-up comedian
- Tour guide
- Voiceover artist

JOB LIST 8

Artisan careers

Before the Industrial Revolution and the spread of mass production techniques, many skills and jobs were passed down through the generations in a guild system; the model of a wise master passing on intricate and secret skills to an eager apprentice in a blissful rural location. There has been a recent revival of this tradition, and many people enjoy deeply rewarding careers within this eclectic field of roles.

Farmers' markets and craft fairs, along with an increased interest in personal health/wellbeing, combined with the increased ease of setting up and running a small business from home, all contribute to the viability of this option. Etsy, an online retailer where producers can sell their handmade products, has 1.7 million active sellers and 28 million active buyers.[20]

As reported by the Governor of the Bank of England, Mark Carney, in 2000, roughly half a billion people had access to the internet. This had risen to three-and-a-half billion people in 2016.

> ... there is an opportunity for mass employment through mass creativity. Technology platforms ... can help give smaller-scale producers and service providers a direct stake in global markets. Smaller scale firms can by-pass big corporates and engage in a form of artisanal globalisation; a revolution that could bring cottage industry full circle.
>
> Mark Carney, The Spectre of Monetarism (Roscoe Lecture)

20 See www.etsy.com/uk/about/.

The meaning of 'artisan' in this book refers to a career you can enter following a specialist course of generally up to a year in which a 'craft' is learned. Categories include:

- Makers and selectors of foods and drinks: chocolate maker, baker, barista, wine producer, cheesemaker
- Handicrafts: needlework, wood turner, potter, joiner
- Arty: photographer, painter

Part 2

What are your job options?

Job options based around teaching skills

This section explores the career options available which retain teaching skills at their core. There are over thirty described here. Many teachers move jobs within this field. Some are reinvigorated by the change and find a permanent niche in which they excel, and others use them as a springboard to further change.

Look through these jobs and highlight any appealing roles. Compare these to the more dramatic changes listed in Part 3.

Twenty career moves you could make if you still want to be a teacher

1   Change class/department

2   Change school

3   Supply teacher

4   Private tutor

5   Change sector (independent school)

6   Change country (international schools in Europe, the Commonwealth, Middle East)

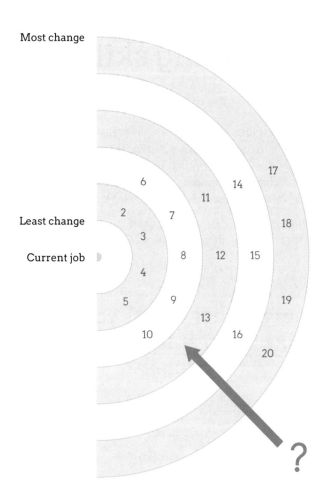

Most change

Least change

Current job

7   Change age range you teach (FE/HE/OU) or train to become a SEN specialist

8   Online teacher

9   Educational writer/editor (websites/publishing)

10 Teacher in hospital/prison

11 Education officer/teacher in a museum or historical site, on a cruise ship, in a resort or theme park

12 Kids' clubs – combine your passion for crafts (e.g. cakes, joinery), music, yoga, sport or science with summer or after-school groups

13 Teaching English as a Foreign Language (TEFL) or English for Speakers of Other Languages (ESOL)

14 Nanny

15 Party event planner/leader

16 Tour guide/ski instructor

17 Motivational speaker to teenagers

18 Trainer to teachers and associated professionals

19 Trainer to adults in a business context

20 Driving instructor

Advice from teachers

I decided to train as a teacher as it had been a career that I'd had in mind for several years and I was fresh out of university with nowhere to go with my psychology degree, without paying to study for my masters. I chose to train as a secondary school English teacher. Big mistake. I enjoyed (and still continue to enjoy) working with older students, but hated the pressure of the subject and the seemingly endless planning and marking out of hours. Basically, I couldn't commit to it 24/7.

My pivotal moment in steering me away from teaching was on parents' evening with the tutor group that I was sharing. I realised that the pastoral side of the job was what I was most enthusiastic about, and I really enjoyed having those conversations with students and parents.

I moved on to a new school and had a year as a cover supervisor, before seeing the advert for my current post. This is my third year as pastoral support manager for Tupton Hall School Sixth Form, and it is quite honestly perfect for me. I have one-to-one interactions with students and parents, dabble in some administrative work and get to work with the teaching staff to ensure that we are supporting the students in all ways. I love my work – and I bet not many people can say that with conviction!

Lucy

'I still like the idea of teaching, but not in my current role'

The smallest change can be within your own school. For some primary teachers, moving from teaching Reception to teaching Year 5 or 6 can have a transformational effect. Even taking on, or being relieved of, responsibility for literacy, maths or a new initiative can make a huge difference. Similarly, there is much scope for secondary teachers to redesign their role within their school. Discuss options with a trusted member of the SLT. With the projected teacher shortages, schools will be looking to support and develop current valued staff, rather than lose them. If you are met with a lack of sympathy or support, that is a massive clue that a change of school could be the best step for you.

If you would like to move between primary and secondary sectors your qualified teacher status (QTS) means you won't need to undertake any further training or do a conversion course.

However, a University Certificate for Returning and Supply Teachers course can be useful for those seeking to move to primary from secondary as a boost to confidence and your CV. Schools recommend that you obtain some experience of the age group you are intending to teach. This could be on a voluntary basis. Some LAs and teacher training institutions offer short refresher and conversion courses.

If you'd like to teach a different subject, you could consider a subject knowledge enhancement (SKE) course which are available for training in biology, geography, maths, physics, chemistry, computing, design and technology, or a language. SKE courses are fully funded, and you may be eligible for a training bursary of up to £7,200 to support you throughout the course. SKE programmes are available all over England at universities and schools, or third parties such as Science Learning Centres. The length of SKEs varies from eight-week refreshers to thirty-six-week courses, offered as full-time classroom-based study, part-time and evening/weekend study, or online.

Advice from teachers

I became a teacher because I wanted to make a difference. I loved teaching, making the ordinary seem extraordinary, and being a positive influence in the lives of the children I taught. I worked long days during the week, regularly roped my husband into my maths marking and spent every Saturday planning or marking. For me, entering the profession with those ideals was unsustainable in the long term for three main reasons. (1) I felt unsupported by senior management: I was denied extra support or resources, despite an influx of children who spoke no English. (2) To progress, I was expected to take on extra responsibility on top of my core work, with no additional non-contact time and for no additional money. (3) Teaching affected my relationships. I had no time for hobbies or interests, and lost contact with friends and family. I felt that I was making a difference to nobody.

I left teaching to become a researcher in a university. It was serendipitous, as they were looking for someone with practical experience in the classroom, were interested in me as I wasn't a traditional researcher, and one of the interview panel had been my dissertation supervisor. It was a huge change moving to the university, and I really enjoyed the academic challenge of researching. I missed the practical link to students, though, and so have since moved to a role within the outreach team where I have more direct contact with schools and students.

My roles in the university have provided me with a much better work–life balance, more scope for professional development, a broader range of career options and, although I miss the classroom, much more job satisfaction.

Kimberley

Small steps you could make include the following.

Supply teacher

Supply teaching can be an excellent short- or longer-term option. Ranging from one-day cover to longer termly placements, roles include primary, secondary, teaching assistant, nursery nurse, school admin and SEN teacher posts. Just like mainstream teaching roles, the work can be equally rewarding and challenging.

The benefits include:

- Freedom from planning, marking and school politics, three of the major causes of teacher dissatisfaction.
- Being able to make a big impact in a short space of time.
- The chance to hone and improve your skills.
- Being able to build towards your long-term career goals.
- The opportunity to earn money while you consider your options.

The challenges include:

- You have to quickly absorb school policies and procedures.
- You must remember where everything is.
- Bonding quickly with new groups of students.
- Developing a set of lesson plans and activities.

The pay varies from £75 to £150 per day. See www.tes.com and Hays.co.uk (worldwide recruiting experts) for more details.

Advice from teachers

I was hoping to return to teaching in my forties after a break to bring up my children. I found jobs always seemed to be offered to people half my age. Thankfully, I have been able to pick up supply work.

Mary

Private tutor

In the run-up to exams and SATs there is a big demand for teachers to tutor students on a one-to-one basis to overcome subject blocks and knowledge gaps. More general revision and learning advice can also prove helpful to parents, as well as their offspring. Tutors often gain great satisfaction from working one-to-one with students. The work is often outside school hours, in evenings and holidays. There are options for tutoring within schools, libraries, playgroups, crafts/music groups, etc. Students with SEN can also require tutors. One advantage of tutoring is that tutors are free from classroom tension/challenges.

Teacher (in another country)

Advice from teachers

I moved to Thailand in 2000 to work at Harrow International School, which is affiliated with Harrow School in London. At that time, Harrow was one of the first independent schools in the UK to franchise across the globe. Thailand may seem a strange destination to begin that process, but in fact the school had an amazing reputation in Thailand. Twenty-seven members of the Thai royal family had previously been educated at Harrow. Previously, I'd worked in a couple of quite challenging inner-city schools. The first and really fundamental difference I found working abroad was that I could actually get on and teach; the students were wonderful to work with and discipline issues were a thing of the past. The second significant difference was the attitude of the Thai community towards education – and indeed teachers, whom they hold in the highest regard. I spent seven great years in Southeast Asia and travelled throughout most of Asia during this time, having some unforgettable experiences for sure.

In 2007 I moved to Bahrain, a small island off the coast of Saudi Arabia, once again to teach at an international school. Unlike Thailand, where most of the students were Thai nationals, the school, which had 2,000 students, boasted over fifty different nationalities. It provided a genuinely international context, and one that my own children thrived in. I often find them on Skype talking to friends around the globe. Of course, there is a significant financial incentive to working in the Middle East too – most schools offer a tax-free salary, free accommodation and utilities, annual flights to the UK and a bonus payment at the end of the contract!

I've moved back to the UK with my wife as our children are at a key transition point in their education. I must admit I've really disliked the first three months back in the UK, but I promised my wife I'd give it a year before complaining. However, our dog loves it here – the first time he ran around in a green park, rummaging nose-deep in all the smells and textures around, I could have cried with satisfaction.

Jason

State sector

The state-maintained sector educates around 85% of all children in the UK. The schools are given a budget, follow a national curriculum imposed by the government and are inspected by Ofsted. There are various versions of organisation structure, such as community schools (controlled by LAs) and others such as foundation schools, trusts, academies, faith schools and free schools (which are controlled by businesses and religious groups). Pupil referral units (PRUs) and special schools are slightly different. Teachers who enjoy this sector are generally attracted by the opportunity of ensuring that all children, regardless of background, have access to a high quality education. Frustrations are often caused by the lack of flexibility within the confines of a rigidly imposed agenda which is unlikely to suit every child (the national curriculum or an academy).

Independent sector (UK)

There are around 2,600 independent schools in the UK. They receive no direct income from the state and have more flexibility in regard to what and how they teach. Members of the Independent Schools Council (ISC) are inspected by their own version of Ofsted. They have their own staff training and development programmes, and do not have to employ staff with qualified teacher status, though most do. Teachers enjoy greater freedom to teach flexibly, often working with smaller class sizes (typically in the low teens). Independent schools with a boarding option (some offer weekly boarding only, while others offer termly boarding), require staff who are interested in pastoral roles. This can be a unique – and rewarding – side to a teaching job. Initially, salaries can be lower, but this can be offset by benefits such as free accommodation.

Independent sector (abroad)

The opportunities to teach abroad are staggering. Education in the UK is generally highly valued across the world despite what PISA surveys may suggest. Many schools abroad cater for UK expats and locals who value the educational offering. Schools often teach GCSEs/A levels as well as the International Baccalaureate (IB) and the US system. This variety can help teachers develop and broaden their pedagogy quickly. Commonwealth countries respect the UK education system and there are currently fifty-three members from Africa, India, Asia, the Pacific and the Caribbean. You don't need to fantasise about teaching in Jamaica, New Zealand, Canada, Malaysia or Mauritius; you can work there. There are also opportunities in all wealthy countries, especially the Gulf states, where salaries can be eye-wateringly attractive.

Advice from teachers

I moved to Dubai in 2008 because my sister was living out here. I was struggling to make ends meet in the UK, teaching on the outskirts of London. I knew I needed to make a change. I'd never considered becoming an expat, though – ironically – I remember someone telling me, while I was training to become a teacher in 2001, that 'the only place you'll ever make enough money as a teacher is in the Middle East'.

My life has changed so much since moving to Dubai. I got married here and both of my kids were born here. I love that this is such a safe place for them to grow up and that they can play safely outside, apart from in the summer when temperatures can reach 50°C!

Teaching in Dubai is amazing. The United Arab Emirates (UAE) is a melting point of innovation and education is a focal point. Every year new initiatives are launched and new opportunities presented. One thing that I love about teaching at an expat school is the diverse range of educators you get to meet, interact with and learn from. It gives you a better understanding of what it means to be a global citizen, and opens you up to new pedagogical approaches that you may not have been exposed to back in your home town. I genuinely learned more about teaching as a profession in my first year out here in Dubai than in the previous five in the UK.

Steve

Teaching a different age group

Some teachers change by teaching a different age group. This is usually fairly seamless within your school: for example, moving from Reception to Year 6 or GCSE to A levels. Moving to an FE college where a wider range of vocational and specialist courses are offered can also change the focus of your teaching: for example, teaching numeracy and literacy to groups of trainee mechanics or beauticians, or maths to adult accounting technicians, will challenge, stretch and hopefully invigorate your work.

Teaching (but not in schools)

Teaching in hospitals, prisons, cinemas, football clubs and even on film sets can be a great way to reinvigorate the most disenchanted and dispirited classroom teacher. A change can be as good as a rest! Teachers working in hospitals describe the special atmosphere in children's wards, which intensifies the emotional pull of the work, making it especially rewarding (and sometimes heartbreaking). Most children will be taught in isolation, although some are taught in groups. At Great Ormond Street Hospital, over 140 children of all ages are taught by thirty teachers in one big room. The Hospital Organisation of Pedagogues in Europe (HOPE) promotes high-quality education in hospitals (see www.hospitalteachers.eu). Hospital schools are governed by the same regulations as all state schools.

To become a film location tutor, you need a licence from your local authority. Pay averages around £150 per day. Be warned: you're more likely to be on a cold set in a wet forest than on the exotic set of *Harry Potter*-style blockbusters.

The Independent Cinema Office (ICO) and Engage support independent exhibitors, cinemas, film festivals and galleries. The British Film Institute (BFI) provides information on vacancies within this sector (see www.bfijobsandopportunities.bfi.

org.uk). Stageworks (see www.stageworksstudio.co.uk) is a source of information.

The WEA offers a range of courses, usually to a mature student group – check out courses run by your local WEA to discover if there are any special interest topics you could teach, such as local history or assertiveness. WEA development officers develop the curriculum, recruit part-time tutors, monitor and evaluate courses, and liaise with local groups.

Prison teachers are usually employed by FE colleges that hold contracts to offer education in a prison or young offender institution. Many staff are employed on part-time contracts. Prison tutors are employed to help offenders with literacy and numeracy to prepare them for being released.

Environmental education officers develop events and learning resources to promote sustainable development. The Council for Environmental Education (CEE) promotes a greater understanding of the countryside through education. The Countryside Foundation for Education (CFE) develops initiatives such as the Growing Schools Programme. This programme delivers a nationwide agenda for outdoor education.

The Federation of City Farms and Community Gardens has opportunities for teachers. The Field Studies Council (FSC), inspired by the natural world, advertises for teachers to work on campaigns, projects and educational programmes.

Music teachers have the option of teaching privately outside the classroom. Mandy Network lists job vacancies, www.mandy.com. Youth Music is a national charity aiming to help young people access opportunities in music, despite coming from more challenging backgrounds. Vacancies and information on their current programmes are available on their website (www.youthmusic.org.uk).

Working with children who have been removed from mainstream or special education is a different environment and a different type of work. **Pupil referral units** generally (and deliberately) don't look like mainstream schools. Some offer residential places. Teachers who can empathise with these children can find this a rewarding career direction.

Some children need to be taught at home and can be supported by a **home teacher**. Experienced teachers usually secure these LA-organised positions.

Or how about **teaching travellers**? There are around 50,000 school-age travellers in the UK. All 150 LAs have Traveller Education Services comprising teachers, classroom assistants and education welfare officers (EWOs). Teaching may be done on traveller sites in converted buses. Positions are often advertised as three-year secondments. Visit www.natt.org.uk (the National Association of Teachers of Travellers) for more information.

Youth offending team workers (YOTs) are tasked with reducing crime by targeting and supporting young people at risk of committing offences. Some teachers develop interventions that steer youngsters in positive directions. Staff work in multidisciplinary teams to ensure services are 'joined up', complementary and effective.

Conductors work at the National Institute of Conductive Education (NICE) and other centres that educate children with movement disorders, such as spina bifida and cerebral palsy.

Portage workers provide home-visiting education support to help train parents to support their own preschool children with developmental or learning difficulties. In-service training is available for people with a relevant qualification, such as QTS.

Curative education professionals work at around forty Camphill Communities (www.camphill.org.uk) across the UK, where they combine the work of a teacher, doctor, therapist and artist to support adults and children with special needs.

Local authorities still offer support services to schools, including pastoral care and training for teachers and school leadership teams, to identify and disseminate good practice. It may be worth checking with your LA to see what sorts of role they may advertise.

SEN teachers specialise in teaching children with emotional, behavioural or learning difficulties. Some work one-to-one with pupils and others work with entire classes. Gain experience and consider relevant roles and responsibilities within a school because these jobs are usually offered to experienced teachers. LAs often run courses that can support progression into roles supporting children with special needs. Specific roles include:

- **Teaching deaf or visually impaired children** – all teachers working with these children must gain a recognised qualification prior to entry or within three years of starting the job. The Royal National Institute of Blind People (RNIB) and Action on Hearing Loss (formerly RNID) websites (www.rnib.org.uk and www.actiononhearingloss.org.uk) list recognised courses which can be full-time, part-time or distance learning. A distance-learning MA qualification is also available for qualified teachers wishing to become teachers of the deaf. You can study while in a teaching post, and bursaries are available.

- **Teaching children with autistic spectrum disorders (ASD)** – there are five specialist residential schools in the UK operated by the National Autistic Society and many others run by LAs for children with ASD. The University of Birmingham offers postgraduate qualifications in autism, including Lovaas training, an applied behaviour analysis technique.

Teaching sports or hobbies

Cycling coach – some LAs are funded to promote cycling in schools.

Fitness instructor/personal trainer – most gyms employ instructors. You can often do this on a part-time or sessional basis.

Yoga teacher – QCF (Certificate Yoga Teaching) Level 3 is the recognised qualification for yoga instructors. Their role covers instruction, guiding and performing. Many are ex-teachers looking for a different pace and focus to their teaching. Some also visit schools to run sessions with groups of children. See the British Wheel of Yoga website (www.bwy.org.uk) for more information.

Martial arts instructor – if you are proficient in one or more of the martial arts, you could consider becoming an instructor. Tae kwon do, ju-jitsu, judo, aikido and karate are the main forms. Each has a national governing body responsible for setting qualification standards. Income is normally per session delivered, and will vary depending on the size of the class and organisation you are working with. For more information see www.sportengland.org.

Sports coach – teachers with a talent for a specific sport have the opportunity to develop it into a career option, teaching individuals or groups. Visit www.ukcoaching.org and select the sport you're interested in from the drop-down list.

Famous people who were teachers before they found fame ...

Gene Simmons – musician

Samantha Harvey – author

Michael Morpurgo – children's author

Sheryl Crow – singer

Joanne Harris – author

J. K. Rowling – children's author

George Orwell – author

Stephen King – thriller writer

Bryan Ferry – singer

Section 2

Job options for recent graduates

If you have recently graduated with a degree plus a PGCE, you can consider competing with current graduates for the many graduate-entry jobs advertised on an annual basis. You can put a positive spin on your foray into teaching and emphasise the transferable skills and knowledge you've accumulated. You have a strong case for proving you have enhanced your communication skills and demonstrated your ability to work under pressure.

One option is to compete for milkround vacancies (the annual trawl of universities made by some of the biggest graduate recruiters). A good year for graduate employment was 2015, with more graduates finding work than in the previous couple of years. Nearly 270,000 students graduated in 2015 – but you're not competing with all of them, as just under half do not enter the job market. The remainder travel, continue studying or take temporary jobs. The Higher Education Careers Services Unit website is an excellent resource for an overview of trends (see www.hecsu.ac.uk). According to their findings, the average graduate starting salary was £20,637 in 2015 and £21,690 in 2016.[1]

The professional careers entered by most graduates were:

- Nursing
- Business
- Human resources and marketing
- Teaching

1   See www.hecsu.ac.uk/current_projects_what_do_graduates_do.htm.

- Programming and software developing
- Finance and investment analysis
- Accountancy (chartered and certified)

If you are interested in any of these areas of work, there are overviews of each in Part 3 of this book. For graduate entry jobs, you could consult the following websites:

www.prospects.ac.uk

www.targetjobs.co.uk

www.milkround.com

www.gradjobs.co.uk

www.reed.co.uk

www.monster.co.uk/graduate

www.graduate-jobs.com

www.jobsite.co.uk/jobs/graduate

The national broadsheet newspapers also have vacancy and career sites for recent graduates.

For a detailed breakdown of graduate entry jobs based on your degree subject, visit www.hecsu.ac.uk/ (and click on 'What do graduates do?').

Jobs linked to your degree subject

To give you an idea of the jobs available, the following section lists ten university subjects and ten jobs that are linked closely to each subject by tasks, skills and knowledge. More details can be found at www.prospects.ac.uk.

Biological sciences

Microbiologist, nature conservation officer, research scientist, soil scientist, laboratory technician, science writer, health promotion officer, landscape architect, town planner, dentist.

Chemistry

Chemical engineer, clinical biochemist, forensic scientist, pharmacologist, toxicologist, patent attorney, scientific writer, accountant, brewer, systems analyst.

Physics

Seismologist, metallurgist, radiation protection practitioner, research scientist, actuary, investment analyst, systems developer, patent attorney, accountant, solicitor.

English

Editorial assistant, journalist, lexicographer, advertising account executive, advertising copywriter, information officer, marketing executive, public relations officer, museum/gallery curator, writer.

Fine art

Advertising art director, fine artist, museum/gallery curator, printmaker, art therapist, arts administrator, TV/film producer, location manager, exhibition officer, multimedia programmer.

Geography

Cartographer, surveyor, town planner, environmental consultant, landscape architect, nature conservation officer, tourism officer, transport planner, logistics and distribution manager, solicitor.

History

Heritage manager, historic buildings inspector, conservation officer, political researcher, museum/gallery curator, academic librarian, information officer, solicitor, exhibition officer, public relations officer.

Maths

Actuary, operational researcher, statistician, accountant, investment analyst/banker, insurance underwriter, ergonomist, economist, research scientist, solicitor.

Modern foreign languages

Interpreter, translator, marketing executive, patent examiner, international aid/development worker, tour manager/guide, event organiser, journalist, location manager, academic librarian.

Sport

Sports administrator, sports coach, fitness centre manager, exercise physiologist, event organiser, health promotion officer, coach, tour manager, broadcast journalist, marketing executive.

Vacancies and internships are advertised at www.milkround. com and you can browse and filter opportunities by start date, location, recruiter type and job title. As a flavour of the range of opportunities available, here are the top twelve out of twenty-four (by numbers of vacancies):

- IT and telecommunications
- Business and management
- Engineering and manufacturing
- Accounting and finance
- Consultancy and strategy
- Marketing and PR
- Construction and property
- Hospitality and tourism

- Sales
- Banking
- Charity and non-profit
- Logistics and transport

The Times and *The Guardian* compile lists of the top graduate employers, which are useful research tools for identifying which companies match your needs.[2] Large banks and accountancy firms feature heavily, but there are also other companies and organisations such as Aldi, the civil service, Tesco, IBM, Marks & Spencer, Arup, GlaxoSmithKline, Accenture and Network Rail, which will each recruit hundreds of graduates each year.

Funding your career change

If you have identified a course and think you might struggle financially to cover fees or living costs, look at the support on offer. First ask the course provider to direct you to potential sources. You may also be eligible for support if you have a strong association to a trade union or organisation with educational, charitable or philanthropic principles.

Bursaries

It's better to identify your preferred career, then research sources of support to fund your training, rather than the other way round. The provider of training will usually be able to offer advice on the support available.

---

2   See M. Birchall, *The Times Top 100 Graduate Employers 2015-16* (High Fliers Publications Ltd, 2015), and https://targetjobs.co.uk/uk300.

There are bursaries available to support people from minority groups to enter professions in which they are under-represented. If this applies to you, it is definitely worth pursuing.

If you're studying a course at a university, it may offer bursaries to cover part of your expenses. The university will point you in the right direction.

For example, if you plan to look for a job in journalism, you could check out:

- NUJ bursaries
- Journalism Diversity Fund (www.journalismdiversityfund. com)
- Guardian Media Group (https://jobs.theguardian.com/ jobs/journalism)

Stipends

If you would like to study for a PhD then most universities will have places available. Full-time courses are generally three years long. Part-time study will generally take six years. Competition for places can be intense and a 2.1 degree is usually a minimum requirement. PhDs offer a route into many jobs within the HE sector. Funding options vary, so check with individual institutions for details. Prospects provides a good startingpoint:www.prospects.ac.uk/postgraduate-study/funding-postgraduate-study.

Grants

The great news is you don't have to pay grants back. Adult learning grants are available for help with childcare, disability needs and so on. Take a look at: www.gov.uk/ grant-bursary-adult-learners.

Educational grants can be found at www.grantsforindividuals. org.uk, although this site charges a fee for access. Ask your course provider if they can search on your behalf on this or from equivalent sources.

Trade unions can offer support through their learning advisers. Unison and Unite both have learning funds.

Loans

You do have to pay back loans, but they can be a way to see you through the training period when financial strain may be greatest.

Career development loans currently allow you to borrow up to £10,000 for up to two years of learning (or three years if the course includes a year of work experience). See www.gov.uk/ career-development-loans/overview.

You could also consider business angels – less scary than those on *Dragons' Den* but they have similar processes and conditions. See www.angelsden.com.

Save for it

An advantage of researching all your options is that you can budget while you're doing it and save for future training.

Job options for school leaders

This section is designed to help experienced teachers, usually those with 'head' or 'senior' in their job title, consider their options. The opportunities already described apply equally to experienced staff, but there are also a few extras worthy of consideration.

Research led by Professor Peter Earley in 2007 discovered that only one-fifth of head teachers who leave their school go on to another headship; around one in eight move into a role within education.[1] The majority retire. Senior staff used to have good pensions to rely upon and could ease themselves into retirement, mixing in a little consultancy, but this is becoming increasingly difficult. Only 5% of teachers aspire to become heads due to the additional workload and poorer work–life balance. There is also the fear that one bad Ofsted inspection will lead to a head's dismissal. Valentine Mulholland, National Association of Head Teachers (NAHT) policy adviser, describes this as the 'football manager's syndrome', comparing head teachers to the only other group of leaders who are individually blamed and brutally dumped following a bad result.[2]

Running a school requires a wide range of skills which transfer across to other leadership and management roles in

---

1 Peter Earley and Dick Weindling, Do school leaders have a shelf life? Career stages and headteacher performance, *Educational Management, Administration and Leadership*, 35(1) (2007): 73–88.

2 Quoted in Rachel Banning-Lover, 60 hour weeks and unrealistic targets: teachers' working lives uncovered, *The Guardian* (22 March 2016). Available at: www.theguardian.com/teacher-network/datablog/2016/mar/22/60-hour-weeks-and-unrealistic-targets-teachers-working-lives-uncovered.

organisations such as other public sector bodies, third sector/not-for-profit and privately owned companies (from small owner managed through to large multinational). As a general rule, if you'd like to specialise in one management function, such as personnel, training or finance, then start with larger companies, but if you like the variety and challenge of being a jack-of-all-trades, then smaller organisations requiring only a few senior positions may be your best starting point.

VSO (Voluntary Service Overseas) offers opportunities to influence education policy, training and delivery in twenty-five countries across the developing world. Head teachers could consider a voluntary or paid position as a way to boost their CV prior to a move into another sector or a role closer to home.

Advice from teachers

I was a head teacher and knew I was ready for a new challenge. I saw a job on a Caribbean island that was for someone to sort out their education system. I applied and got the post. It was an exhilarating job in which I really made an impact. I identified key areas for improvement, including teacher training and school starting age, and went for it. After five years I returned to the UK and now I'm head of a nursery school and run a training and advice support service in early years across Lincolnshire. I do think too many teachers stay put and would benefit from a change.

Kate

The school leadership cycle

There is a natural cycle to all jobs, and experienced senior leaders could consider the cycle described by Professor Tim Brighouse as a four-stage, eight-year cycle of initiation, development, stall and decline.[3]

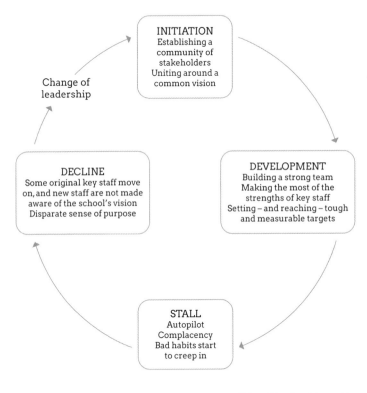

INITIATION
Establishing a community of stakeholders
Uniting around a common vision

Change of leadership

DECLINE
Some original key staff move on, and new staff are not made aware of the school's vision
Disparate sense of purpose

DEVELOPMENT
Building a strong team
Making the most of the strengths of key staff
Setting – and reaching – tough and measurable targets

STALL
Autopilot
Complacency
Bad habits start to creep in

School leadership cycle

3   Tim Brighouse, *How Successful Head Teachers Survive and Thrive* (Abingdon: RM Education, 2007). Available at: http://support.rm.com/_rmvirtual/Media/ Downloads/How_head_teachers_survive_and_thrive_by_prof_Tim_Brighouse. pdf.

Many teachers enjoy the excitement and energy of the first two stages and become bored once all the hard work of turning around a failing school or completing a challenge has been done. If you are in this place in the cycle, move on to another challenge before governors or others decide you are in the 'stall' or 'decline' phase, and relieve you of your duties and/or career in an ungrateful, damaging and demeaning manner.

Analyse your strengths as a leader to help you see where you could be successful in future. All organisations require staff in senior roles to be adaptable and have many positive qualities. As a head, you are usually responsible (and accountable) for these. In many organisations these functions are split.

Professor Tim Brighouse identifies six key tasks of lead teachers and leaders in *How Successful Head Teachers Survive and Thrive*. Which of these are you?

Energy creator

Generating a passion for success.

Spreading optimism across the whole school and in stakeholders.

Building a 'what if?' rather than a 'this is why we can't' approach.

Skills builder

Building capacity and skills of the SLT.

Fostering a 'we' rather than a 'them and us' environment.

Vision builder

Uniting everyone around a shared vision.

Identifying obstacles and dealing with them quickly.

Environment builder

Ensuring all supplies and equipment are fit for purpose.

Making the environment a positive and pleasant place to be.

Staff leader

Seeking and leading improvement.

Comparative benchmarking.

Appreciative enquiry.

Extending the vision

Adapting and tweaking the vision to suit the journey of the school and the stakeholders.

Being aware of external threats and opportunities.

Advice from teachers

Over ten years I had worked my way from humanities teacher to vice-principal in a small secondary school in a challenging area. The school merged with others and became part of a chain. Following the inevitable staff restructuring, I lost my job. I'd given so much of myself to the school that I felt betrayed. When I thought about the things I'd enjoyed most, I remembered an initiative I had been involved with in which we supported a group of students to develop their confidence and ability in maths. After a little research, I discovered that my maths A level, plus a conversion course at Tower Hamlets College, meant I could return to the classroom as a maths teacher. I've been teaching maths for a year now, and it is challenging but rewarding.

John

It may also be useful to contact some executive recruitment agencies. They will quickly match your skills and experience to potential employers and vacancies. Some may be able to help you present yourself appropriately to employers in other sectors. They can save you a lot of time, thanks to their knowledge of the employer and their exact requirements, as well as updating you on any developments in the field you need to know about.

Commercial organisations offering consultancy services (such as recruitment, training, purchasing and quality control) to schools, LAs, universities and colleges could be an interesting move for senior teachers.

Networking your way forward

One of the most effective tools for career success is often kept quiet. This is ironic, as it's networking. If we are all six degrees of separation from each of the nearly seven billion people on this planet, then the power of networking is surely one to focus on.

The major benefits of networking are that it's easy to start, not as time consuming as traditional job application processes, and it can lead you in new and unexpected directions. As well as expanding your knowledge of the opportunities out there, it develops key skills such as researching, telephone technique and interviewing professionals. The only real drawbacks are that it's a long-term investment (so start now, as well as researching other ideas) and that you'll be occasionally knocked back or rejected. A good starting point is to list your existing network. This includes family, friends, neighbours, past employers, colleagues and union representatives. What could you ask each of these people? Teaching can make teachers think they should know all the answers. Networking can be a liberating experience, allowing you to rejoice in discovering answers from others.

Part 3

Job profiles

This section contains around one hundred jobs presented as alternatives to teaching. These have been chosen to represent the wide range available.

The jobs cover different levels – some need minimal or no additional training, while others involve lengthy postgraduate qualifications.

The jobs cover different sectors – teaching and training, performing, social care, technical and therapeutic medical care, artisan roles, business administration and management, working with animals, flexible working and self-employment.

Jobs across all levels of income are included.

There are many more opportunities. If you can't find something that catches your interest here, then you can use this list as a way to identify some of the factors that are important to you. Choosing a career is a bit like choosing a partner – a bit of compromise helps. No partner[1] or job is perfect – plus, once you make the choice there will be some pleasant and unexpected experiences along the way and, if it doesn't work out, it's usually easier to go back to a previous job than a previous partner.

---

1   Other than mine, if she's reading this.

Limbering up for careers guidance

The process explained

> It's like being your own life detective ... no one is more expert on bringing happiness into your life than you are.
>
> Liz Hoggard, *How to be Happy*, p. 33

Some things to think about before you start

Make a list of all your interests and hobbies here.

....

....

....

....

....

....

Could any of these be turned into jobs?

Some will require a little extra training (such as barista or prison officer) and others lengthy additional training (such as dentist or psychologist). The rest will require something in the middle (such as marketing executive or air traffic controller).

For how long could you afford to retrain?

Do you need a salary? If yes, then part-time training is the answer. If no, you have more options.

How to use the job profiles

Each job profile gives information on the job, the tasks involved in the job, entry routes into the job, salary, key roles and websites that will provide more information. These factors are discussed in greater depth below.

The information included in the job profiles section has been gathered from many different sources. In addition to the websites referred to in each profile, the following sites are also recommended as sources of thorough job information:

https://nationalcareersservice.direct.gov.uk

www.prospects.ac.uk

www.agcas.org.uk

Brief overview of the job tasks

Would you enjoy some or all of these options? Tick or add a smiley face to the jobs you like the sound of, and put a cross or sad face by those you don't like the sound of. This will help you compare jobs later on.

Entry routes

Here, we refer to specific qualifications and skills required for entry. Will you need to retrain? How much will it cost? Can you train part-time, via distance learning, or locally?

Salary

Typical salary information is presented, usually per annum. Most ranges are large and depend on location and size of company. Generally companies in London/the south-east of England and larger organisations offer higher salaries. Do factor in the type of contracts offered and other perks. A lower paid permanent contract could be better than a short-term or fixed-term contract on a higher salary.

Key roles

Remember in Part 1 when I asked 'Who are you?' I asked you to circle the words that appealed to you most – bear in mind these preferences as you look through the options in this section. Three key roles are included for each job. Do these match your career preferences?

Still interested?

This section gives web-based sources of more detailed information about the work and sources of vacancies for each job.

Let's start with an example: the (almost real) job of 'celebrity'.

Celebrity

There are four legal ways to become a celebrity:

1 Contributing something worthwhile to society and sharing it through selected media outlets.

2 Dating a celebrity and spilling the beans to the tabloids.

3 Creating a YouTube hit (possibly featuring your baby laughing, your cat singing or your dog roller-skating).

4 Applying for a TV show featuring the public (*The Voice, The X Factor, Big Brother, Gogglebox, Coach Trip, Don't Tell the Bride*, etc.).

Salary: It is traditional to earn a vast wodge of cash when you first become a celebrity, only for it to dry up spectacularly after your fifteen minutes of fame. Your life is then basically ruined by tabloid reporters sifting through your bins, tutting their way through your empty wine bottles and asking students you used to teach to say mean things about you. However, the working hours are generally good and you will have time to watch the trashy day-time TV programmes you used to guest on, unless you land a minor panto role in a bleak northern seaside town, which will make you doubt everything positive you have ever believed and yearn for a teacher's life.

Key roles: performer, entrepreneur, source of public contempt/derision.

Still interested?

www.bbc.co.uk/showsandtours/takepart – BBC

(This entry is deliberately included for a bit of fun, so please don't roast me on Amazon or Twitter!)

Accommodation manager

Universities, care homes, hospitals, hotels and housing associations all have managers to run their accommodation and manage the wide range of staff working to clean and maintain the buildings. They are responsible for budgets, staff training and liaising with staff in other management functions. Depending on the size of the employer, salaries can range from £20,000 to over £40,000. Postgraduate qualifications such as an MBA in Hospitality Management can be studied in-post.

Key roles: strategist, manager, communicator.

Still interested?

www.caterer.com – The Caterer

www.instituteofhospitality.org – Institute of Hospitality

Job area: Accountancy

Accountant

Accounting technician

Internal auditor

Accountancy is a major employment sector in the UK and thousands of graduates enter the profession annually. This could be a great move if you have:

- Numerical and quantitative skills.
- An analytical and problem-solving approach.
- Good negotiation and communication skills.

- The dedication and transferable skills developed within teaching.

To become an accountant you need a professional accountancy qualification offered by ACCA (Association of Chartered Certified Accountants) and CIMA (Chartered Institute of Management Accountants). These are usually studied for in-post. You can also work your way up through the AAT (Association of Accounting Technicians) route. The Institute of Chartered Accountants in England and Wales (ICAEW) offers a three- to five-year training scheme, the ACA (Association of Chartered Accountants) qualification, for graduates based in a firm. Once qualified, there are opportunities in banking and finance, business, consulting and management. The cliché that accountants have to work really hard to qualify is certainly true, but the cliché that the work is dull is certainly not, as accountants can branch out in many directions within all sectors of business and internationally.

Salaries can be among the highest for professionals, starting at around £30,000 and rising to £50,000 per annum. The average annual salary in business is over £90,000, with banking and capital markets attracting higher salaries. People attracted to teaching are generally not motivated by high salaries alone, and there are ways to make other contributions using accountancy skills, such as working for ethical organisations, charities, non-governmental organisations and so on. Other related professions such as **actuary** (they evaluate, manage and advise on financial risks using models based on economics, probability theory, statistics and investment theory) are also worthy of consideration.

For some career changers, a better option is to research specialist jobs within a sector, with a salary and on-the-job training, rather than the professional-level job that requires longer training. In the financial sector, two such opportunities are **accounting technician** (AT) and **internal auditor (IA)**. Both roles involve similar work and skill sets to those of an accountant, but they specialise in one area. ATs earn from £16,000 per annum during training, rising to over £30,000 once qualified. Progression to professional qualifications then becomes an option. IAs work within companies to assess performance, identify risk and assess the impact of new projects and policies. On-the-job training to complete Chartered Institute of Internal Auditor qualifications is available, and salaries are usually similar to those of ATs.

Key roles: inspector, manager, strategist.

Still interested?

www.icaew.com – Institute of Chartered Accountants in England and Wales

www.wibf.org.uk – Women in Banking and Finance

www.aat.org.uk – Association of Accounting Technicians

www.iia.org.uk – Chartered Institute of Internal Auditors

Actor

Many teachers channel their inner actor during their classroom work. If you'd like to go a step further, then read on. Research by Drama UK discovered that 86% of actors in work have had professional training – see www.federationofdramaschools. co.uk. Acting courses do not have an upper age limit. As it is such a competitive career choice you could start with short courses or evening classes to check out your level of desire and commitment to the calling. Postgraduate acting diplomas are available, and some bursaries and scholarships are offered (see the Federation of Drama Schools website, below). The work requires talent, stamina, persistence, punctuality and discipline. Salaries vary for theatre, live performance, film, TV and radio.

Key roles: communicator, creator, performer.

Still interested?

www.federationofdramaschools.co.uk – Federation of Drama Schools

www.equity.org.uk – Equity

Administrator

Not all teachers are from the Christopher Biggins and Brian Blessed school of communication. A high proportion of teachers enjoy working on tasks and projects quietly, efficiently and without fuss and fanfare. Administration jobs allow these skills to shine through.

Perhaps you could start your search across all education sector companies and employers, as they employ many administrators in various roles. You could also target companies of special interest to you, such as the National Trust, donkey sanctuaries or local companies.

 Key roles: inspector, supervisor, manager.

 Still interested?

www.totaljobs.com – Total Jobs

www.nationaltrustjobs.org.uk – National Trust

Adventure travel guide

Few jobs can combine the application of inspiration and organisation skills in such a spectacular way as this role. If you'd like to escort and lead groups of families, friends, solo travellers or business team-building groups on organised adventures, then this could be an ideal career move. Trips could be as varied as walking in the Alps, a Serengeti safari or a polar expedition. You can incorporate your interests and skills, such as kayaking, cave exploration, scuba diving, sailing or canoeing. You could be responsible for organising accommodation, meals and first aid. Salaries can vary greatly, but the majority of posts will be between £14,000 and £24,000 per annum.

Key roles: explorer, guide, leader.

Still interested?

www.familyadventurecompany.co.uk – Family Adventure Company

www.exodus.co.uk – Exodus Travels

www.intrepidtravel.com – Intrepid Travel

www.wildfoottravel.com – Wildfoot Travel

Advice worker

Advice workers provide face-to-face, telephone- or IT-based free, impartial and confidential advice to people on issues such as debt, housing, training and employment, welfare and education. Work may involve liaising with other organisations on behalf of clients, setting up support groups, researching and preparing reports on hot topics. Salaries are likely to be between £16,000 and £25,000 per annum. Training is generally undertaken in post rather than prior to entry. Many people start on a voluntary basis, and contracts are often short-term or temporary. Advisers report that the work is incredibly rewarding and often stressful, as genuine demand for support outstrips the resources available.

Key roles: advice, advocate, guide.

Still interested?

www.citizensadvice.org.uk – Citizens Advice

www.jobsinadvice.org.uk – Jobs in Advice

http://jobs.thirdsector.co.uk – Third Sector

Air cabin crew

Teachers who are seeking a change of direction – literally – could consider working in a growth industry such as air travel. Ensuring a wide range of passengers have a comfortable and safe flight is the focus of the work. Salaries are generally low, and you can expect to earn between £15,000 and £25,000 per annum. Perks such as free flights can ease the pain of a lower salary. Entry requirements vary between airlines, although good health, a second language and an absence of visible tattoos are fairly standard requirements. There are a number of other posts available at airports. Many airlines are big employers: for example, British Airways employs over 40,000 people, and offers graduate programmes across a wide range of management and technical roles.

Key roles: helper, guide, organiser.

Still interested?

www.careersthatmove.co.uk – Careers that Move (People 1st)

https://jobs.ba.com/jobs – British Airways

Air traffic controller

Air traffic controllers work at airports, directing aircraft during landing and take-off and flights within UK airspace, handling over two million flights each year. They work shifts, on a forty hours per week basis. The work requires great attention to detail and procedures, clear communication skills and high levels of concentration. Income starts at around £32,000, rising to £50,000 for experienced staff. Training involves gaining an approved air traffic control licence which takes six months – for example, with NATS (formerly National Air Traffic Services). NATS's website includes games to assess your skills to discover if you have what it takes. Although the training is relatively quick, the entry process can take a few years. One person in every 150 applicants makes it through the process to become qualified and employed. Academic entry qualifications are five A–C grades at GCSE, including maths and English, which should be no problem for teachers. You must also be physically fit.

Key roles: manager, strategist, protector.

Still interested?

www.nats.aero – the main air navigation service provider in the UK

http://jobs.flightglobal.com – the best aviation and aerospace jobs, courses and careers advice

www.raf.mod.uk – Royal Air Force

Alternative education teacher

There are many people who reject the focus of today's education system on tests, exams and conformity. Parents with alternative views often seek schools with a like-minded philosophy to educate their children. If the philosophy of a decentralised school (which is more child- than system-focused, and aims to develop creativity and a love of learning) appeals to you as a teacher, then Montessori, Steiner Waldorf or Human Scale Education could be for you.

Still interested?

www.freedom-in-education.co.uk – Freedom in Education

www.montessori.org.uk – Montessori Education

www.steinerwaldorf.org.uk – Steiner Waldorf Schools Fellowship

Art/drama/music therapist

In this job, you will create a secure environment in which activities are used to build the confidence and self-awareness of young people, adults or the elderly with emotional, behavioural or mental health problems, learning disabilities, neurological or physical illnesses. The work is one-to-one and group-based in the NHS, social services, education and/or prison settings.

Postgraduate art therapy courses are two years full-time or three years part-time study. A first degree in art is desirable. A short introductory course run by the British Association of Art Therapists (BAAT) can help you decide if this is the right career move for you.

Drama therapy uses role play, voice work, movement and storytelling to explore and resolve personal and social problems. A postgraduate course taking between one and three years is required. A relevant first degree and experience would be useful.

Music therapy uses live musical experiences to improve clients' wellbeing. Postgraduate training of between two and four years follows a music degree as the entry route. For all three roles, registration with the Health and Care Professions Council (HCPC) is required.

Key roles: healer, inventor, performer.

Still interested?

www.baat.org – British Association of Art Therapists

www.badth.org.uk – British Association of Drama Therapists

www.bamt.org – British Association for Music Therapy

Advice from teachers

I trained as a dancer at Laban (now Trinity Laban) and did some professional dance work. I didn't intend to become a teacher, but started dance teaching to supplement my income and loved it. I did my Cert Ed at Goldsmiths. Perhaps the pivotal moment of my career was working at Camden School for Girls. I was tasked with introducing and championing dance within the school, including a new GCSE course in dance to achieve timetabling parity with other subjects. I had a huge amount of freedom and support – a great combination for a young, enthusiastic and passionate teacher. Following the birth of my first daughter, I job-shared and lost some of the control on which I'd thrived. I left work after the arrival of my second daughter, intending to return. Instead I taught creative dance classes to very young children. This led to work at my children's primary school one day per week teaching dance to KS1 and 2 children. I then worked for The Place, a conservatoire of dance and home of the Richard Alston Dance Company, in primary schools across London. A project exploring dance as a multisensory learning approach led me and a partner to my current role, which is running a business training teachers to use dance in their schools. The work I do is incredibly rewarding. I've found a niche that works for me professionally and personally, a challenge faced by most women with families.

Alison

Bingo caller

Bingo callers work across the UK in large bingo chains, independent clubs, holiday camps and on cruise ships. If you are lively, witty, outgoing, a confident presenter, have clear pronunciation and understand the rules, then this could be the career for you. Salaries tend to range between £12,000 and £18,000 per annum; however, the best callers can be poached by rivals.

Key roles: communicator, performer, improviser.

Still interested?

www.bingo-association.co.uk – Bingo Association

www.nationalbingo.co.uk – National Bingo Game

British Sign Language (BSL) interpreter

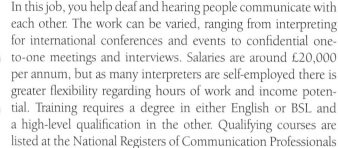

In this job, you help deaf and hearing people communicate with each other. The work can be varied, ranging from interpreting for international conferences and events to confidential one-to-one meetings and interviews. Salaries are around £20,000 per annum, but as many interpreters are self-employed there is greater flexibility regarding hours of work and income potential. Training requires a degree in either English or BSL and a high-level qualification in the other. Qualifying courses are listed at the National Registers of Communication Professionals working with Deaf and Deafblind People (www.nrcpd.org.uk).

Key roles: guide, communicator, helper.

Still interested?

www.actiononhearingloss.org.uk – Action on Hearing Loss

www.ibsl.org.uk – Institute of British Sign Language

Care assistant

A common question asked by career-changers is: which job sectors are guaranteed to grow over the next few years? It can be difficult to predict future trends, but it's a safe bet that the number of care assistants is likely to increase as our population ages. More people are cared for in their home or in community settings. Current predictions are that there will be a need for a staggering 200,000 extra care workers by 2020. Roles include working with children, those with physical or learning disabilities and the elderly. The work is varied, but likely to include activities such as daily personal care, housework, food preparation, paying bills, writing letters and organising leisure activities. Liaison with health professionals, social workers and local authority staff (housing, benefits) is also an important part of the job. Salaries are low for the nature and importance of the work. Many people will be working at minimum wage level. Salaries can rise to over £20,000 per annum for senior positions. A good starting point is voluntary work, and staff report that the work is rewarding and not as traumatic as supporting a close family member.

Key roles: carer, protector, advocate.

Still interested?

www.skillsforcare.org.uk – Skills for Care

Careers adviser

Careers advisers support individuals to make course, training and career decisions. They work in universities, the National Careers Service, schools, colleges, charities and organisations supporting unemployed/vulnerable people into employment. There are also positions available in some larger companies/ organisations. They work mostly one-to-one with people, providing a mix of information, advice and guidance. Talks and presentations to groups can also be part of their work, as well as visits to employers and providers of education and training opportunities. Providing specialist support to clients with specific needs, such as mental health issues or physical disabilities, is also an option. Training, via NVQ levels 2 to 6, can be on the job or prior to entry. Salaries vary greatly (from £15,000 to £30,000 per annum), and are generally commensurate with qualification levels required for posts.

 Key roles: adviser, guide, advocate.

Still interested?

www.thecdi.net – Career Development Institute

www.agcas.org.uk – Association of Graduate Careers Advisory Services (AGCAS)

Chauffeur

As a chauffeur, you drive clients to and from places. You can work exclusively for one client or for a specialist company dealing with many clients (hotels, tour operators, personal security companies, large organisations). Hours are likely to be unsociable. Salaries are generally somewhere between £15,000–£25,000 per annum.

 Key roles: organiser, protector, guide.

Still interested?

www.britishchauffeursguild.co.uk – British Chauffeurs Guild

Children and family court advisory and support service worker

The Children and Family Court Advisory and Support Service (CAFCASS) is a non-departmental government body. Workers support children's and their parents' interests in family proceedings to ensure they are heard and the decisions made are understood.

Four roles exist:

- **Children and family reporters** specialise in working with children of divorcing/separating parents,
- **Children's guardians** work in cases involving social services and contested adoptions,
- **Reporting officers** ensure parents understand the adoption process and what is being consented to,
- **A guardian ad litem** is court-appointed. They mediate between parents who are unable to reach agreement.

A degree in social work is usually required for these posts. Salaries start at around £18,000 per annum. See the CAFCASS website for vacancy details.

Key roles: counsellor, adviser, organiser.

Still interested?

www.cafcass.gov.uk – Children and Family Court Advisory and Support Service

Children's rep (tour operator)

The job involves organising a range of activities for children aged between three and twelve.

A preparatory online course is available (www.holidayrepdiploma.co.uk). The work is demanding, but it's an opportunity to create fun and creative learning experiences without Ofsted and predicted test scores at the back of your mind. Salaries are likely to be low, but accommodation is included in most instances. An adventure and a useful addition to your CV could await.

Key roles: supervisor, helper, carer.

Still interested?

Check the websites of major tour operators such as Thomas Cook (www.thomascook.com) and Thomson (www.thomson.co.uk) for vacancies and training details.

Chocolate taster

If your mouth is watering by the time you finish the following list of potential employers then this may be your dream job: Green & Black's, Cadbury, Hotel Chocolat, Nestlé, Thorntons.

A master chocolate taster, spending 10–20% of their time tasting chocolate and the remainder mixing and testing new product ideas, can earn up to £30,000 per annum for manufacturers such as Mondelez (owner of the Cadbury and Kraft brands). Having a science degree or food industry experience (such as being a chef) would be an ideal background. If you can't land this dream job, there are options as a food judge/consumer tester in which, as part of a panel, you will provide feedback on new products (including the sound of the chocolate as it snaps, and its 'melt in the mouth' properties) and taste combinations to support the professionals back in the laboratory.

There are other options if chocolate isn't your thing. Tasters are required for all types of food. Everything found in a can or plastic package is tasted. Some people are even employed as dog food tasters! Companies such as Thorntons and Hotel Chocolat offer retail roles at their high street outlets.

Key roles: inspector, inventor, creator.

Still interested?

Contact the manufacturers of your favourite brands for more information.

www.hotelchocolat.com/uk/careers

http://thorntons.networxrecruitment.net
www.nestle.co.uk/careers

Circus performer

If you are physically fit, coordinated and enjoy learning new skills then this could be your next career move. Training is offered on short courses, master classes, summer schools and workshops by providers such as Circus Maniacs, the Academy of Circus Arts and My Aerial Home. Performers are usually paid per show, at a rate between £200 and £1,000. Street theatre, festivals, parties and corporate events offer more work than traditional circuses.

Key roles: performer, improviser, comedian.

Still interested?

www.creative-choices.co.uk – Creative and Cultural Skills
www.nationalcircus.org.uk – National Centre for Circus Arts
www.equity.org.uk – Equity

Clown

OK, if you're adding your own jokes here or pulling faces, then this might actually be the job for you. There is more to clowning than you might think. Some clowns work in healthcare environments to help vulnerable people (combining many techniques which could be labelled classroom craft, including improvisation, music and rhythm, song, dance, magic, puppetry, games and storytelling). Indeed, there is a tradition within all cultures throughout human history of clowns, or tricksters, who inspire people by appearing to be a fool or comic character. Learning the art form is possible via introductory weekend courses that invite you to connect to your playful spirit, or lengthier courses with a Nose to Nose training programme. From flexing your teaching skills in new ways in schools, to building your business training bankers to love more than cash, there are a number of ways to turn your natural clown into a satisfying career path.

Key roles: improviser, comedian, magician.

Still interested?

www.heartsminds.org.uk – Hearts and Minds

www.nosetonose.info – Nose to Nose (clowning website)

Cognitive behavioural therapy (CBT) practitioner

Talking therapies are playing an increasingly important role within the NHS and outside it. They focus on how people think about things in their life that could have an impact on their wellbeing. CBT is used to help people with panic disorders, anxiety, depression or obsessive-compulsive disorders. Clients can be referred privately or through the NHS. Working within hospitals, as part of community mental health or psychotherapy departments, is possible. The work involves talking one-to-one with clients over a series of meetings, with the intention of alleviating symptoms or creating new, more helpful beliefs. Great communication skills, empathy, problem-solving skills and the ability to work as part of a team are essential. Some

group work is possible. Salaries are generally between £26,000 and £31,000 per annum. The most senior posts can command

salaries of over £80,000 per annum. Entry is usually via a relevant degree such as nursing, social work or psychology, followed by an accredited postgraduate CBT qualification, which takes between one and three years. However, teachers may be able to demonstrate that they have key knowledge, skills and interests for entry to the postgraduate courses.

Key roles: healer, adviser, communicator.

Still interested?

www.iapt.nhs.uk – Improving Access to Psychological Therapies

www.healthcareers.nhs.uk – Health Careers

www.babcp.com – British Association for Behavioural and Cognitive Therapies

www.bps.org.uk – British Psychological Society

Comedian

A steady stream of teachers move from standing in the corner of a classroom to standing in the sticky-floored corners of small pubs and converted church halls. Famous names such as Greg Davies, Frank Skinner, Romesh Ranganathan and Sue Smith are outnumbered by many other ex-teachers who make a living from the comedy industry. If you have ten minutes of material, you will find open mic spots at venues across the UK. You can try it out, and if you like the buzz – and audiences like you – then you have your foot in the door. Apparently you need the audience to laugh four to six times per minute, and they should laugh for 20 seconds of each minute. Roughly one in a hundred wannabe stand-ups make it through this stage. Most comedians advise getting on stage to learn about your act, as it's a 'learn by doing' art form. Many performers combine their stand-up with other employment, such as hosting corporate events, as the chance of earning a living exclusively from paid gigs is remote. However, you could channel your poverty and unsocial working hours into your act.

Typical salaries after a couple of years on the circuit are £20,000 per annum, rising to £50,000 for the most established performers. There are more opportunities to work in larger cities where there tend to be more comedy clubs.

Key roles: comedian, communicator, performer.

Still interested?

www.jongleurs.co.uk – Jongleurs (comedy clubs)

www.hilaritybites.co.uk – Hilarity Bites (comedy clubs)

Top tips from Dave Keeling, stand-up comedian and educationalist

Start keeping a note of things you find funny or make you laugh (this could include quotes, sayings, stories, incidents, words that sound funny). Always attempt to write about stuff you know – this will help you to find your 'voice' [a term used to describe your style of delivery].

Be unafraid to fail. Every comic who has ever stood up has fallen flat on their backside at least once during their career. As a stand-up, the first thing you must develop is a thick skin and a bouncy bottom! Each gig should be viewed as an opportunity to learn, develop and improve. Try it out, cock it up, then try it differently. If it doesn't work a third time, let it go and move on.

I would recommend booking a comedy course. Not only are they reasonably priced, but they allow you space and time in a supportive environment to try stuff out before you unleash it on the public. You will also be surrounded with other budding comics who are going through the same experience. Most courses culminate with a comedy night, saving you the trouble of having to find your first gig. Until you have actually stood up on stage and had a go, you'll never know if it's for you – or not.

Community education coordinator

Community education coordinators ensure that appropriate education, training and recreational courses are available for their local community. They also encourage participation, can recruit tutors, liaise with current education providers and bid for funding. They need to be great networkers and administrators, and be positive about the power of education to develop the confidence, motivation and skills of the groups with which they work, such as families, minority groups, unemployed people or teenagers. They also need good organisational skills.

Salaries are around £25,000 per annum. Employers can include local education authorities (LEAs), housing associations, the National Youth Agency, FE colleges, the Workers' Educational Association and YMCA. A third of positions are part-time.

Key roles: organiser, catalyst, advocate.

Still interested?

www.et-foundation.co.uk – Education and Training Foundation

www.nya.org.uk – National Youth Agency

Complementary and alternative medicine practitioner

Teachers considering moving into jobs helping people via medical intervention could consider complementary or alternative medicine (CAM). If you don't believe in CAM, then look instead at traditional NHS roles or other careers.

Although often used as a single heading, there are differences in how the treatments are used. They can complement NHS treatment under guidance from the National Institute for Health and Care Excellence (NICE) (such as the Alexander technique for Parkinson's disease, or acupuncture and massage for spinal and persistent lower back pain). Or they can be an alternative, possibly standalone, treatment provided by osteopaths and chiropractors. The Complementary and Natural Healthcare Council (CNHC) is the UK regulator of complementary therapies. Its website can help you identify the range of jobs available. Registered therapies currently include the Alexander technique, massage therapy, naturopathy, reflexology, reiki and nutritional therapy.

An interest in human biology, anatomy and health, plus good communication and listening skills, are central for CAM practitioners.

Acupuncturists discuss symptoms around lifestyle, diet and emotions, and diagnose areas of the body to insert needles, with the intention of relieving symptoms and restoring health and energy. Common conditions treated using acupuncture include migraine, arthritis, high blood pressure, depression and addiction. Training is a three-year course. Clients usually pay £40–£100 per hour, but the therapist won't necessarily receive 100% of this if they work through an agency or rent their treatment space.

Alexander technique teachers assess and improve posture and coordination, including voice/breathing problems, to improve individuals' physical and mental wellbeing. They deal with a wide range of people including music and drama students, pregnant women and athletes as well as private clients. Training is a three- to four-year course. Income will be around 60% of the £50–£100 per hour paid by clients, if the therapist has to pay a cut to a third-party.

Chiropractors manipulate the soft tissue, bones and joints to prevent injury or reduce pain in the neck, back, shoulders and legs. They sometimes diagnose issues using blood tests and X-rays. Training takes four years. Salaries range from a cut of the £40–£80 per hour paid by clients to £30,000–£80,000 for those running a successful practice.

Osteopaths use touch and manipulation to reduce swelling, ease pain and increase mobility around muscles, bones, nerves and joints. Clients include older people with arthritis and athletes. Training is a four-year degree course. Clients will pay up to £50 per session.

Other therapies include colour therapy, homeopathy and reiki. You can make up your own mind about the efficacy of these options by visiting the sites below.

Key roles: healer, helper, entrepreneur.

Still interested?

www.icnm.org.uk – Institute for Complementary and Natural Medicine

www.cnhc.org.uk – Complementary and Natural Healthcare Council

www.acupuncture.org.uk – British Acupuncture Council

www.paat.org.uk – Professional Association of Alexander teachers

www.gcc-uk.org – General Chiropractic Council

www.osteopathy.org.uk – General Osteopathic Council

Conference and exhibition organiser

Could you organise and run events, exhibitions, trade shows and conferences? Excellent communication, organising, budgeting and sales skills are essential. The work can involve researching levels of interest in new concepts, booking additional contributors, finding suitable venues, coordination of marketing and promotion, selling space and generating press/ media interest. Salaries are likely to be in the region of £20,000 to £40,000 per annum. On-the-job qualifications in events and hospitality management are available. Contacting companies involved with the many education-based shows and conferences would be a logical starting point for teachers. There are growing opportunities for international travel as part of this role. Universities and some other large companies sometimes employ their own in-house conference teams.

 Key roles: supervisor, entrepreneur, catalyst.

 Still interested?

www.aceinternational.org – Ace International (global market research company)

www.abpco.org – Association of British Professional Conference Organisers

Crossword compiler

Scottish insect travelling in time with Mr Fox (five letters)?[2]

Crossword compilers really enjoy their work.

Although it's a spare-time job for most compilers, there is an opportunity to make this a full-time occupation if you have the interest and dedication in setting crosswords and other brain-teasers, anagrams and puzzles. Ex-teacher Sue Purcell works for Puzzler, the organisation responsible for many UK magazines and supplier of puzzles for print and online providers. She advises people against this career move if they want to earn a huge salary. Have a go at setting a crossword to see if this would suit you.

 Key roles: writer, improviser, creator.

Still interested?

www.puzzler.com – Puzzler (contains a selection of the crossword books, Sudoku puzzles and others on the market)

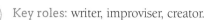

2   McFly.

Doctor

It isn't uncommon for people to train to become a doctor as a second career. Due to the lengthy training involved, medical schools are sympathetic to those who have gained experience in another career before committing to medicine. To qualify you must complete a degree in medicine recognised by the General Medical Council (GMC). These take five years. Science graduates with a 2:1 and a good A level grade in chemistry can apply for a four-year Graduate Entry Medicine (GEM) degree at thirteen UK universities. A six-year alternative for non-science graduates is available at seven universities, although two still require A level chemistry. You may be asked to complete a UK Clinical Aptitude Test (UKCAT) to check your suitability, as well as being assessed on your academic background. Financial support for medical degrees is currently available towards the end of your training, but you're likely to build up substantial debt. Then, there is a two-year foundation programme in which you work in a range of clinical settings. Further specialist training in your chosen area, such as paediatrics, cardiology or general practice, completes your journey. The work is equally demanding and rewarding. Opportunities across the world are available to qualified and experienced doctors, with flexible and part-time working hours possible. Salaries during training start at around £23,000, rising to £30,000 per annum during specialist training. Experienced specialist doctors will earn over £80,000 per annum.

Key roles: healer, advocate, sage.

Still interested?

www.healthcareers.nhs.uk – Health Careers

www.bma.org.uk – British Medical Association

www.gmc-uk.org – General Medical Council

Dog handler

Working with a specially trained dog, you would be part of a team helping to prevent or detect crime, search for lost or missing people, control crowds or guard prisoners. You would be responsible for the care and control of your dog. You need patience and confidence. Most dog handlers are employed by the police, army, Royal Air Force, UK Border Force or private security firms. Entry and training depend on the employer you choose. Police officers and armed forces personnel transfer to the dog section after three or so years. The National Search and Rescue Dog Association (NSARDA) requires experience as a full-time member of a mountain or lowland rescue team. Private security firms and companies set their own entry requirements. For people who love dogs, can work with minimum supervision, possess good observational skills and thrive in pressured situations, the work can be immensely rewarding. You could also consider being an unpaid dog (or cat) fosterer, caring for rescued animals as part of their rehabilitation – contact the RSPCA (www.rspca.org.uk/home) for further details.

 Key roles: instructor, explorer, inspector.

Still interested?

www.gov.uk/government/organisations/border-force – Border Force (part of Home Office)

www.sia.homeoffice.gov.uk – Security Industry Authority

http://recruit.college.police.uk – College of Policing

Driving instructor

Teaching people to drive can be interesting, varied and stressful work. Driving skills, patience and excellent communication skills are the essential attributes. The work has many parallels with classroom teaching, both in the learning journey of the learner and the building of confidence and skill.

The main differences are working with people of all ages and backgrounds, and the opportunity to be self-employed. Most instructors work evenings and weekends. To qualify as an approved driving instructor (ADI), you must be over 21 and have held a driving licence for over three years without serious convictions. The ADI exam has three parts, comprising knowledge, practical driving skills and teaching ability. Many people start working with a franchised driving school earning up to £300 per week. Established instructors generally earn between £25,000–£30,000. This is a job in which you can decide on your own working hours.

Key roles: instructor, organiser, entrepreneur.

Still interested?

www.driving.org – Driving Instructors Association

www.careersthatmove.co.uk – Careers That Move

www.gov.uk/guidance/official-register-of-driving-instructor-training-ordit-scheme#ordit-membership-first-inspection-and-entry-onto-the-register – Official Register of Driving Instructor Training

Education officer

Teaching in a different setting is an ideal solution for many teachers frustrated with their current environment. Education officers (EOs) can be found in a diverse range of locations and organisations. Think of something you are passionate about, and there is likely to be an EO somewhere responsible for spreading that passion to others. Some cinemas and theatres employ EOs, and the British Film Institute and National Theatre are great sources of vacancies. Zoos and wildlife parks, sporting clubs or bodies (football clubs, rugby) also offer opportunities. Community and family EO roles also exist.

Key roles: teacher, performer, creator.

Still interested?

www.bfi.org.uk – British Film Institute

www.nationaltheatre.org.uk/learning – National Theatre

www.ncsthechallenge.org – National Citizen Service

Educational psychologist/child psychotherapist

Both of these roles assess and treat children who are experiencing problems detrimental to their learning. They will work with multidisciplinary teams, training and advising other professionals involved in education, and developing supporting courses and materials for teachers and parents. Salaries are initially equivalent to teaching scales, but increase for experienced staff to be equivalent to, or exceed, senior teaching positions.

Educational psychologists – if you don't have a psychology degree you can do a British Psychological Society (BPS) conversion course, followed by a doctorate (teachers can be awarded exemptions from parts of the course). Funding for fees can be available from LAs for all three years of the course.

Child psychotherapist – this is an established second career for teachers. Psychotherapists treat issues such as depression, phobias, anxiety, self-harm and eating disorders. Lengthy training is also involved. The Association of Child Psychotherapists (ACP) and the UK Council for Psychotherapy (UKCP) offer accredited courses that can take six years to complete.

Key roles: healer, counsellor, strategist.

Still interested?

www.gov.uk – search for 'Educational Psychology Funded Training Scheme'

www.bps.org.uk – British Psychological Society

www.childpsychotherapy.org.uk – Association of Child Psychotherapists

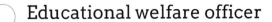

Educational welfare officer

Educational welfare officers (EWOs) work with students, schools, social services, educational psychologists, court staff and parents to positively influence attendance. Working with children individually in a supportive role can be so different to the classroom experience that many teachers are rewarded in a way they weren't as teachers. Salaries are comparable to teaching scales, between £22,000 and £30,000 per annum. Youth and community work or social work qualifications are useful, but may not be required for fully qualified teachers. Employers are either local authorities or groups of schools. Volunteering in youth work can be a great way to dip your toe in the water and decide whether the pastoral and mentoring roles appeal to you.

Key roles: helper, mentor, organiser.

Still interested?

www.lgjobs.com – Local Government Jobs

EFL teacher

Also known as TESL, TESOL and ESOL. This involves teaching adults whose first language isn't English, to help with their work, education or preparation for a UK entry test. Lesson preparation, creating learning resources, setting and marking work are the main tasks. Income can range between £15,000 and £25,000. A qualification in addition to PGCE may not be essential, though Cambridge CELTA and Trinity CertTESOL (certificates in Teaching English to Speakers of Other Languages) are the most commonly recognised. Course lengths vary from four weeks (full-time) to one year (part-time). There are opportunities to work across the world for qualified and experienced teachers. For a list of UK-based accredited schools, see the British Council website (www.britishcouncil.org).

Key roles: teacher, improviser, performer.

(i) Still interested?

www.trinitycollege.com – Trinity College London

www.iatefl.org – International Association of Teachers of English as a Foreign Language

E-learning developer

This work encompasses the natural skill set and interest profile of the majority of teachers. Developers primarily design and prepare course materials, activities and resources that can be accessed online. This is a growing sector. As the demand for podcasts, webcasting and videoconferencing increases, so does the need for more developers. The work can include using web-authoring software, moderating interactive discussion areas, liaising with tutors, managing user accounts, creating or modifying video/audio clips and giving presentations. You can be employed directly by larger companies or external consul-tancies. Work is office-based, within a forty-hour Monday to Friday working week. Salaries are generally around £25,000 per annum, rising to £35,000 for senior developer posts. Relevant qualifications are a degree in computing, multimedia design, teaching or educational technology. Promotion and specialist roles include research, strategy planning, educational software design and computer gaming.

(K) Key roles: manager, trainer, creator.

(i) Still interested?

www.thetechpartnership.com – Tech Partnership (skills for the digital economy)

https://moodle.org – Moodle (open source community)

Equalities and diversity officer

This job involves promoting equality and diversity within an organisation, through research, developing and introducing new policies, preparing and coordinating events such as Women's Week, checking organisational information to ensure it meets equal opportunity standards and delivering training and information sessions to groups. Experience of promoting equal opportunities is useful, and is something which could be developed while a teacher. Posts are generally within large companies and public sector bodies such as the Crown Prosecution Service, prisons or LAs. Salaries are within the range of £18,000 to £40,000 per annum. Further training is available once you are in post.

Key roles: advocate, organiser.

Still interested?

www.cipd.co.uk – Chartered Institute of Personnel and Development

www.equalityhumanrights.com – Equality and Human Rights Commission

www.equalityanddiversity.co.uk – Equality and Diversity UK

www.diversitylink.co.uk/diversity_equality_jobs.php – portal for equality and diversity managers in the UK

Estate agent

Estate agents and modern teachers have much in common. Both need to be clear and confident communicators with people from all backgrounds, well organised and able to make progress with challenging targets. Both work in cut-throat, results-driven industries. Estate agents can enjoy the personal financial rewards resulting from their hard work in a way that is impossible for teachers in schools. Salaries can start as low as £15,000 (rising to £25,000) before commission on sales is included. When the property market is booming (or you are based in London), the earning potential is better; when the property market is going through a downturn, you will earn less. Industry-recognised qualifications are available by distance learning or part-time study for staff covering property sales, lettings, management and auctioneering.

 Key roles: organiser, guide, advocate.

 Still interested?

www.naea.co.uk – National Association of Estate Agents

www.rics.org/uk – Royal Institution of Chartered Surveyors

Exam marker (in the UK)

This role could be a great way to boost your income and your continuous professional development (CPD).

The main boards, the Assessment and Qualifications Alliance (AQA), Edexcel and OCR require excellent teachers to set and mark their examinations. If you're a qualified teacher with three terms of recent teaching experience within the subject and level (GCSE, A level, etc.), you can apply. You can expect to earn between £500 and £1,000 per season, roughly one or two weeks over summer, as a new marker. This can increase significantly as you gain experience and mark more complex papers and attend meetings.

If this is supplementing your teaching, the impact on your practice can be positive. You will see how students behave in exams and apply this knowledge to help your own students' performance. You could also share tips and knowledge with your colleagues and the parents of your students. Your grade predictions are likely to be more accurate.

Associated roles as examiners, standards verifiers and moderators also exist.

 Key roles: teacher, inspector, supervisor.

Still interested?

www.aqa.org.uk – AQA exam board

www.ocr.org.uk – OCR exam board

www.pearson.com/careers.html – Pearson

Firefighter

This is a stressful, physically demanding, rewarding and varied position, including putting out different kinds of industrial and residential fires, rescuing people from danger, advising on safety, plus speaking to groups, including schools. Full-time and part-time (retained) posts exist. Salaries start at around £30,000 per annum. Each fire service sets its own entry requirements. Contact the chief fire officer in the area you would like to work.

Key roles: warrior, protector, inspector.

Still interested?

www.fireservice.co.uk – Fire Service resources

www.nwfs.net – Women in the Fire Service

Foster carer

Each day in the UK over 60,000 young people are being cared for by foster parents. Although not necessarily a traditional career choice, fostering can be a rewarding option. There are a number of different placement types in which you support children who are unable to live with their own families. You could offer:

- Short-term placements for children while their needs are assessed, or long-term placements for children who are unable to return to their own family.

- Regular or one-off short-term placements with children to give their family or longer term foster parents a break.
- Specialist placements (generally requiring extra training) for more complex cases, such as supporting a parent as well as their child, or children with disabilities.
- Refugee placement (an area of increasing need).

The motivation to foster is similar to teaching: the desire to make a positive difference to the lives of young people. It requires patience, flexibility and being able to work with a wide range of professionals. Practical requirements vary, but generally include the following: you must have a spare bedroom, a driving licence and car, and if you are part of a couple you must have been together for more than two years. The process of becoming a foster carer is fairly lengthy, to ensure you are able to support the children placed with you. Training and support networks are in place to help you be successful in the role. Fosterers are financially recompensed, ranging from £150 to £500 per child per week. The vote to form a foster carers' trade union in 2016 suggests the work is moving to a more professional 'job' role with contracts, rights and protections.

Key roles: helper, mentor, carer.

Still interested?

www.fostering.net – The Fostering Network

www.teamfostering.co.uk – Team Fostering

www.thefca.co.uk – Foster Care Associates

Funeral director

Funeral directors guide bereaved people through the process of organising a funeral, sensitively and professionally. Compassion and organisational skills underpin this work, as coordination of timings and details such as flower collection, transport, preparing the body and arranging memorials such as headstones have to be right first time. Salaries are likely to be between £20,000 and £30,000 per annum. On-the-job training is available, including a Diploma in Funeral Arranging and Administration and a Diploma in Funeral Directing. Vacancies are advertised in the trade magazine *Funeral Director Monthly*.

Key roles: supervisor, manager, inspector.

Still interested?

www.nafdqualifications.org.uk – National Association of Funeral Directors

www.bifd.org.uk – British Institute of Funeral Directors

Health promotion specialist

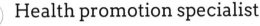

It's a cliché that we have a National Sickness Service rather than a National Health Service. The focus on the promotion of healthy lifestyles and diets to delay or prevent illness is a relatively new departure for the NHS. If you are tactful, persuasive and can motivate people to make positive changes, then this can be very rewarding work. You should also be prepared to practise what you preach and embrace healthy lifestyle choices. Good organisational skills are essential as you will juggle various working commitments. As well as working with individuals, you may also be involved in wider public health campaigns, local and regional policy development, developing partnerships with other stakeholders, researching and producing materials, and running training courses and workshops. The main salary scale is between £22,000 and £28,000 per annum, with a scale of between £31,000 and £41,000 per annum for experienced staff. A relevant degree, such as psychology or sports science, is useful. Experienced professionals, including teachers, can enter health promotion as a second career and gain qualifications in-post. The Open University offers a Certificate in Health Promotion. Most posts are within the NHS, but some voluntary, charitable and international groups recruit health promotion specialists.

 Key roles: communicator, adviser, healer.

 Still interested?

www.healthcareers.nhs.uk – NHS Health Careers

www.rsph.org.uk – Royal Society for Public Health

Higher education lecturer

As well as teaching, most lecturers are involved with research. If you'd really like to become an expert in your degree subject and retain a teaching role (involving teaching large groups, smaller seminars and some individual student support), then this could be a great match for you. You'll probably need a 2:1 in your degree and have, or be working towards, a PhD. You could start further training, part-time, while in your current post. Salaries are generally higher than the teaching scale. They start at £33,000 and rise to £55,000 per annum for senior lecturers.

 Key roles: teacher, communicator, creator.

Still interested?

www.heacademy.ac.uk – Higher Education Academy

Hypnotherapist

Hypnosis is used to help clients overcome a range of conditions, including phobias, anxiety, sleep problems, stress-related conditions, to manage pain and change bad habits such as smoking, nail-biting or overeating. Generally therapists work individually with clients. Most are self-employed, and many combine other professional backgrounds such as nursing or counselling with hypnotherapy, earning £50–£100 per session.

Training can vary in length; short introductory courses can act as a taster experience (an ideal way to help you decide if this is a career option you'd like to pursue). Teachers could specialise, for example, to help teenagers with exam anxiety or other issues related to teenage or educational experiences. You can combine hypnotherapy with CBT and mindfulness training.

 Key roles: healer, communicator, entrepreneur.

 Still interested?

www.hypnotherapists.org.uk – National Council for Hypnotherapy

www.nationalhypnotherapysociety.org – National Hypnotherapy Society

www.ukhypnosis.com – UK College of Hypnosis and Hypnotherapy

Insurance claims handler

You will liaise with policyholders to check the validity and accuracy of claims made, coordinate tradespeople and replacement goods, and arrange payments following accidents or burglaries. Visits to various sites, liaising with legal professionals, keeping accurate records and handling any complaints associated with a claim are some of the main tasks you will undertake. Some larger insurance companies offer graduate entry management training schemes. Salaries for trainee positions are around £20,000, rising to £50,000 per annum for senior staff. Loss adjuster, health and safety inspector, insurance broker, insurance risk surveyor and insurance underwriter positions may also appeal.

Key roles: inspector, adviser, strategist.

Still interested?

www.cii.co.uk – Chartered Insurance Institute

www.cila.co.uk – Chartered Institute of Loss Adjusters

Inventor

The inventor is a very British stereotype. For every *Dragons' Den* wannabe, there are thousands of people developing products and service ideas linked to their passions for niche or mass markets. You could be inspired by your teaching experiences, a hobby or a poor customer service experience.

Debbie Sterling, a toy inventor from the United States, was an engineering student frustrated that toys for girls excluded building and engineering sets. She researched the market and developed GoldieBlox. The project set involves the child making things for the character Goldie so she can help her friends – such as a machine to help her dog chase its tail, requiring the construction of a belt drive. Manufacturers and companies were initially sceptical about her product, but an internet-based marketing launch helped propel her business into a successful series. The mix of skills required to take a product to market can help everyone find their niche within the business world, even if their product is ultimately unsuccessful.

 Key roles: inventor, entrepreneur, improviser.

Still interested?

www.innovate-design.co.uk – Innovate Product Design

Journalist

Teachers have many of the core skills required to excel in journalism: outstanding written and verbal communication, good research skills, incisive questioning, listening and tenacity. It is also a career with a level of excitement and variety on a par with teaching. The traditional route into journalism is a fourteen- to twenty-two-week fast-track course or one academic year, part-time postgraduate course. These are either pre-entry (you attend a course run by a training organisation or college and fund it yourself; some bursaries are available) or direct entry courses (you obtain a position with a newspaper group and they train you). Peter Barron, *Northern Echo* editor, advises applicants to the regional press to be aware of the paper's successful campaigns and best exclusives. Entry is highly competitive, so provide strong evidence of your writing skills, come prepared with ideas for stories and their visual treatment, and be able to film and edit your own video content and add graphics to stand out. Journalists usually work for about two years before branching out into a specialist role, such as editing, public relations work or areas of interest such as sport, politics, law, travel, magazine, online content or broadcast journalism.

Do you have curiosity hardwired into your DNA, coupled with a passion for finding, telling and sharing stories? These are the qualities sought by Mark Wray, head of training at the BBC.[3]

If you are a blogger or specialist magazine article writer, there is a possibility you could start earning without formal training. Contact potential recipients of your output to gauge their level of enthusiasm for your insights. Salary scales are on a par with main teaching scales. Trainees generally earn around £15,000, and senior journalists can earn up to £50,000.

Key roles: communicator, writer, explorer.

Still interested?

www.newsmediauk.org – News Media Association

www.nctj.com – National Council for the Training of Journalists

www.bjtc.org.uk – Broadcast Journalism Training Council

www.nuj.org.uk/work/training – National Union of Journalists training

www.pressgazette.co.uk/jobs – Jobs4Journalists

....

3   Press Gazette, *How to be a Journalist 2015/16* (London: Press Gazette in association with the National Council for the Training of Journalists, 2015). Available at: https://issuu.com/press_gazette/docs/trainingguidefinal_hires_p5_v3, p. 16.

Laboratory technician

A move to a familiar role within a school or other educational or research company, without the increased responsibility of teaching, can be a welcome change. Duties include setting up experiments and recording results, monitoring and ordering stock, supporting individual students with their research (in HE) and assisting teachers/lecturers. Salaries are likely to be in the £15,000 to £20,000 range, and posts are advertised on school or FE/HE vacancy sites.

Key roles: inspector, organiser, helper.

Still interested?

www.ase.org.uk – Association for Science Education

www.cleapss.org.uk – Consortium of Local Education Authorities for the Provision of Science Services

Learning mentor

Mentors help students deal with any difficulties they have that are impacting their education. Issues you can help alleviate include erratic attendance, low confidence, problems settling in, bullying and bereavement. The work will involve one-to-one support, home visits and liaising with other professionals such as social workers, educational psychologists and education welfare officers. Work is often during normal school hours, although some after-school support may be required. Vacancies are available in the full range of educational settings: schools, FE colleges, special schools, universities and some companies and trade unions. Salaries start at around £15,000 and can rise to £25,000 per annum. Each LEA sets its own entry requirements, but it is unlikely that qualified teachers would not be welcomed as applicants.

Key roles: mentor, guide, instructor.

i Still interested?

www.lgjobs.com – Local Government Jobs

www.feadvice.org.uk – FE Advice (information about the FE and skills sector)

Librarian

There is a pleasant overlap of duties in librarian and teaching roles. As well as running a university, college, company or public library, the job can involve working with groups of library users, setting up reading groups, preparing displays, organising community events, research and teaching research skills. Salaries are most likely to range between £20,000 and £30,000 per annum. The availability of postgraduate qualifications mean entry for teachers can be relatively smooth.

Key roles: instructor, communicator, guide.

Still interested?

www.cilip.org.uk – Chartered Institute of Library and Information Professionals

www.lisjobnet.com – Library and Information Jobs

Licensed conveyancer

In this job you will liaise with a wide range of people, both in person and on the phone/via email. It requires great communication, people and organisational skills. As a property law specialist (working in England and Wales), the bulk of your work will be in dealing with legal matters, and the administration and finance associated with buying and selling property (residential/business) and land. During training, salaries are likely to be under £20,000 per annum but once you are qualified and experienced they can rise to £50,000 (depending upon region and type of employer). To practice, you must pass the Council for Licensed Conveyancers (CLC) qualification, which takes two to four years under the supervision of a solicitor. Employers include solicitors, property firms, LAs, banks, building societies and civil service departments.

Key roles: inspector, communicator, manager.

Still interested?

www.clc-uk.org – Council for Licensed Conveyancers

www.lawgazette.co.uk – Law Society Gazette

Life coach

Life coaches help people identify their goals and develop a plan to reach their goals using their current resources and skills. Teachers may be familiar with the model used, as it is often adopted in the classroom to motivate students. The work is mostly with individual adults. Life coaches tend to earn between £30 and £60 per session. Coaches to managers in business can charge four-figure sums per hour! The work sounds easier than it is. Good coaches need to be excellent communicators, combining tact, tenacity and attention to detail. Part-time training courses are available, and can be useful personal development (an opportunity to coach yourself!) as well as a career move.

Key roles: guide, strategist, communicator.

Still interested?

www.cipd.co.uk – Chartered Institute of Personnel and Development

www.coachingnetwork.org.uk – Coaching and Mentoring Network

Local authority school support officer

Local authorities still offer services to schools, including pastoral support, training for teachers/school leadership teams, and identifying and disseminating good practice. Specific job roles such as home education and teaching the children of travellers are featured elsewhere.

Key roles: supervisor, manager, adviser.

Still interested?

Have a look at your LA's website for a snapshot of the opportunities available.

Marketing executive

As a marketing executive, you are responsible for promoting the products, services or ideas of a company. Qualities such as organisation, research, creativity and networking skills are at the heart of this work. Working for an organisation with beliefs and values that match your own can be very rewarding. Salaries start at around £20,000, rising to £40,000 per annum. Marketing directors can command salaries over £50,000 per annum. In-post qualifications from the Chartered Institute of Management (CIM) and the Communication, Advertising and Marketing Education Foundation are available.

Key roles: communicator, creator, strategist.

Still interested?

www.cim.co.uk – Chartered Institute of Marketing

www.theidm.com – Institute of Direct and Digital Marketing

www.a-m-a.co.uk – Arts Marketing Association

Martial arts instructor

If you are proficient in one or more of the martial arts you could consider becoming an instructor. Tae kwon do, ju-jitsu, judo, aikido and karate are the main forms. Each has a national governing body responsible for setting qualification standards. Income per session delivered is unlikely to exceed £100.

Key roles: instructor, trainer, entrepreneur.

Still interested?

www.sportengland.org – Sport England

Motivational speaker

Using your teaching skills to motivate and inspire teenagers, in school or when they're out at conferences, exhibitions or university visits, is a job that can be seamlessly combined with other options, such as a teacher-trainer or other positions linked to education, private tutoring, blogging and writing. Is your own life story motivational? Can you mine your subject specialism or a hobby/interest to create an engaging presentation? Sir Ken Robinson spoke at business conferences and events about his passion to embed creativity in education for many years before his famous TED Talk made him an international speaker.[4] You could volunteer to deliver at TeachMeet events or on INSET days to discover if the work appeals and to hone your craft.

Key roles: performer, catalyst, sage.

Still interested?

www.sfb.com – Speakers for Business

4   See www.ted.com/talks/ken_robinson_says_schools_kill_creativity?
    language=en.

National Citizen Service worker

The NCS organises 'once in a lifetime' summer placements for fifteen- to seventeen-year-olds across England. It is a government-backed programme. The work involves supporting and inspiring teenagers during residential experiences. Salaries are often between £1,200 and £1,500 per month on contracts that can be as short as one month. Over 38,000 teenagers took part in summer 2016 programmes. Some posts involve speaking to groups of pupils in schools to make them aware of the opportunities available and sign up those interested. The role can include all the administration associated with the programme.

Key roles: teacher, performer, motivator.

Still interested?

www.ncsyes.co.uk – National Citizen Service

NHS clinical scientist

There are a number of professional medical roles within the NHS that are less well known than doctors, nurses and thera-pist roles. They require a degree in health care science via the NHS Scientist Training Programme (STP), which includes work-based training in a range of settings followed by the choice of a specialism for the final two years. The course is available to sci-ence and engineering graduates with a 2:1 or first-class degree. Roles include clinical bioinformatics, clinical immunology, microbiology, biomechanical engineering, nuclear medicine, physiological sciences, audiology, sleep science and MRI/ultra-sound. Posts can be lab-based or patient-focused.

Salary scales are from £22,000 to £28,000 for newly qualified staff.

Key roles: inspector, manager, supervisor.

Still interested?

www.healthcareers.nhs.uk – Health Careers

Nurse

Nursing encompasses a number of specialist roles, including adult nurse, mental health nurse, paediatric nurse and general practice nurse. Related jobs include health visitor, speech and language therapist, health promotion officer, occupational therapist, counsellor, dietitian, midwife, paramedic and radiographer.

To work as a nurse in the UK, registration with the Nursing and Midwifery Council (NMC) is required. To qualify, you must complete an NMC-approved degree course. You choose one of four specialisms (adult, children's, learning disability or mental health, though you can change area after qualification). Good health and relevant work experience are required, along with evidence of a skill set typical of teachers (communication, empathy, sensitivity, flexibility, the ability to work well in a team and organisational skills).

Nurses are paid on national scales starting at £22,692 and rising to £28,180. Senior positions are on a higher salary band which reaches £35,000. Nurse consultants can earn up to £67,000 per annum. Additional specialist training is available, such as cardiac nursing, infection control, theatre and recovery.

Key roles: healer, helper, organiser.

Still interested?

www.healthcareers.nhs.uk – Health Careers

NVQ assessor

This job involves supporting people who are gaining their national vocational qualifications while employed. This can involve visiting individuals in their place of work as well as delivering some training to groups at a central location. The job involves much of what many teachers say is the most rewarding part of the teacher's role: building the confidence and skills of individuals as they progress towards their goals. This is often part of a role involving other teaching duties. Salaries start at around £18,000, rising to a maximum of £30,000 per annum.

Key roles: inspector, mentor, instructor.

Still interested?

www.feadvice.org.uk – Further Education Advice

Ofsted inspector

Is it poacher turned gamekeeper – or the other way round? If you're a teacher, you will be familiar with the role of Ofsted inspectors in schools. Ofsted provides similar functions within the social care and Early Years education sectors. Changes in 2015 have meant the number of school HMI inspectors has been cut and they are now employed centrally to improve the consistency of services offered. Inspectors are normally outstanding teachers with a track record of success in senior roles and a familiarity with the latest policies and procedures filtering down from the government. The recruitment process starts with an online application form, which is assessed by your HMI peers. The next step is an interview and presentation tasks, plus a panel interview chaired by the regional director. If you agree with Amanda Spielman's vision for state education, then you're in – if you don't, and want to overthrow the system from within, then best of luck. Salaries start at £64,000 per annum.

Key roles: catalyst, inspector, strategist.

Still interested?

www.ofsted.gov.uk – Ofsted

Online teacher/tutor

This involves preparing learning materials, offering email support, delivering face-to-face tutorials by video conferencing/Skype, and setting up student forums and chat rooms. Virtual teachers share the same skill sets as classroom-based teachers, and must also be computer-savvy. Qualifications in e-learning (such as Learning to Teach Online) are useful, but not essential. Recruitment procedures and the advertising vacancies vary between distance learning companies, so it is best to approach each directly. Correspondence schools can rely totally on speculative applications. Salaries range from £13,000 to £24,000 a year.

Key roles: teacher, organiser, writer.

Still interested?

www.openstudycollege.com – browse this online directory of distance learning courses to identify the courses you would like to teach. You can then contact the providers to offer your services.

Job area: Open University

With more than 200,000 students, the Open University (OU) is the UK's biggest university. It is a world leader in flexible part-time education, often pioneering in its use of the most up-to-date technology and distance learning. As well as undergraduate and postgraduate courses, the OU offers informal and free learning globally.

The OU employs 11,000 staff, and around half of these are associate lecturers.

 Key roles: teacher, organiser, advocate.

Lecturer/senior lecturer

Lecturers develop and deliver high-quality distance learning modules and materials, including online forums and tutorials. They also contribute to departmental research and the training and supervision of associate lecturers. The majority of posts are based in Milton Keynes, Buckinghamshire. The working environment is flexible and collaborative. New staff are inducted into the unique OU teaching process. Permanent staff are offered two months' paid study leave (per two years). Vacancies are plentiful and varied due to the size of the OU. For example, at the time of writing, vacancies in the following subjects were being advertised: statistics, twentieth-century European history, biology, health sciences, mathematics and finance. A PhD is essential for most posts, as well as a track record of successful research design and delivery. Salaries are within the range of £32,000 to £55,000 per annum.

Associate lecturer

Many professionals work part-time as associate lecturers. Posts that only involve online support have no geographical restrictions. Posts with face-to-face student support are linked to twelve regional centres. The www.open.ac.uk website allows users to search for vacancies by faculty and location. For example, if you taught the module 'Investigating Psychology', you could have fifteen students in your group each submitting five assignments for 60 credits towards a degree. You would work for six hours per week between October and June. The salary band is very broad, ranging from £1,200–£7,000 per module.

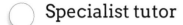

Specialist tutor

These posts are to support student teachers to engage with the open learning dimension of the OU's Initial Teacher Training programme.

Research associate

Research associates work within departments, including Arts and Humanities, Design, Languages, Medical Sciences, Education, Childhood and Youth, Computing and IT, Engineering and Psychology and Counselling.

Dynamic and highly motivated individuals, preferably with a PhD, are required to research topics that are funded externally or internally. Salaries are around £33,000 as part of fixed-term contracts.

If you are considering studying for a PhD, the site www. postgrad.com is a good starting point.

Support staff

There are a large number of non-academic staff working at OU centres across the UK. Roles in administration and professional support include: curriculum assistant, student recruitment, project officer, business development manager, careers adviser, strategic analyst. You can browse current vacancies at www. open.ac.uk/about/employment/.

Key roles: communicator, inspector, organiser.

Still interested?

www.open.ac.uk – Open University

Outdoor activities instructor

This work aims to build people's confidence, motivation and social skills. You can lead team-building days for companies, leisure activities open to the public or activity-based courses for disadvantaged youngsters. Like teaching, the work involves planning, delivering, recording student progress, assessing health and safety, and evaluating courses. The most common activities are climbing, canoeing, skiing, snowboarding and hill-walking. You can work abroad in holiday resorts or in centres throughout the UK. Qualifications are available for each activity, and include the Mountain Leader Award, the British Canoe Union (BCU) Certificate in Coaching Paddlesport and the UK Snowsports Coaching Awards scheme. More details about courses and jobs are available from the Institute for Outdoor Learning (www.outdoor-learning.org). Salaries are fairly modest, rising to £25,000 per annum for leader and manager posts.

Key roles: teacher, trainer, instructor.

Still interested?

www.skillsactive.com – SkillsActive

Paramedic

Paramedics attend medical emergencies. They are often the first to arrive, and quickly assess injuries and provide treatment such as resuscitating patients, using a defibrillator, applying splints, and administering oxygen and intravenous drugs. Calls can range from minor accidents to major transport accidents. Salaries are on a scale ranging from £21,500 to £28,000, while senior positions attract higher salaries. Entry is either via an approved university course in paramedic science or by applying to an ambulance trust for a student paramedic position (with on-the-job training).

Key roles: explorer, protector, healer.

Still interested?

www.hpc-uk.org – Health and Care Professions Council

www.collegeofparamedics.co.uk – College of Paramedics

Police officer

Modern policing requires confident, proactive, physically fit and resilient people able to communicate effectively and flexibly with a range of people. The work may be closer to teaching than it was in the past. There are forty-three police services in the UK, including the British Transport Police and Civil Nuclear Constabulary, and each recruits its own staff.

Salaries range from £19,000 to £50,000. Police officers with several years' experience are likely to earn around £35,000 per annum.

Key roles: protector, inspector, communicator.

Still interested?

www.sfjuk.com – Skills for Justice

www.police.uk/contact/force-websites – a list of all police force addresses

Prison officer

Prison officers supervise inmates in a prison, remand centre or young offender institution. Working with people in difficult circumstances requires a blend of patience, compassion, firmness, attention to procedural detail and emotional resilience. The entry process starts with a Prison Officer Selection Test (POST) which checks numeracy, reading and writing skills. An assessment and selection day follows which assesses personal qualities and physical fitness. If selected, an eight-week entry-level training course must be completed, which covers professional standards, team-building and interpersonal skills, interviewing and report writing, security, searching and con-trol/restraint techniques. Salaries start at under £20,000 but rise to £30,000 per annum for experienced staff. Work usually involves night and weekend shifts.

Key roles: protector, communicator, supervisor.

Still interested?

www.justice.gov.uk/jobs/prisons – HM Prison Service

Private tutor/Learning centre owner

There are a growing number of individuals and companies offering private tutoring to children and adults, across all curriculum and subject areas. The majority of opportunities are to help people prepare for important key educational transition points such as SATs, entrance tests, GCSE and A level examinations. The most popular subjects are maths and English. For a private tutor visiting children in their own homes, income generally starts at between £10 and £25 an hour. This is an easy career move to sample, by simply asking around friends and family to identify a guinea pig. Flex your teaching skills to assess an individual and prepare a bespoke learning programme for them. If you enjoy the work, you can expand your number of tutees by advertising locally. Some groups, such as Kumon and First Class Learning, offer franchising opportunities. For an initial fee of £7,000, you can build a successful business tutoring children in your area. First Class Learning has over 200 franchisees. The model runs like a private gym where parents pay a monthly fee for their children, usually around £50 per subject, to access tutor support at a town centre location. You benefit from access to professional support, marketing and resources. You could work at one of these groups as a tutor to assess whether the ethos and approach matches your own.

Key roles: teacher, entrepreneur, manager.

Still interested?

www.childcare.co.uk/find/Private-Tutors – childcare website on which you can search for tutors/register as a tutor

www.firstclasslearning.co.uk – First Class Learning

www.kumon.co.uk – Kumon

Probation officer and probation services officer

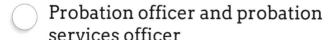

The National Probation Service is currently undergoing major reorganisation. The work itself, however – reducing crime by supporting offenders – remains constant. Supervising people serving community and prison sentences by building strong relationships through interviews with offenders and associated professionals is at the core of the work. Tasks include assessing risk, preparing court or parole reports, delivering individual and group support, arranging training, housing or drug/alcohol treatment, and supporting victims of crime. A probation services officer (PSO) earns around £25,000 per annum, or up to £22 per hour if working on a temporary contract, and works with lower-risk offenders than a probation officer (PO). For a PSO post, experience (paid or voluntary) of working with offenders in any of the following settings – hostels, victim support services, youth offending teams or prison visiting – is useful. PSOs apply in-post to become POs, who can earn up to £35,000. To be eligible to take a Graduate Diploma in Community Justice (to become a PO), you need a degree involving at least 50% criminology, police studies, community justice or criminal justice.

Key roles: guide, mentor, advocate.

Still interested?

www.traintobeaprobationofficer.com – National Probation Service

www.sfjuk.com – Skills for Justice

Professional speaker

There are many different ways to earn your living by speaking to groups. They include conferences, exhibitions, trade shows, INSET days, after-dinner speeches and talks to specialist groups such as children, parents, teachers and other professionals with an interest in education. This is a niche for teachers with charisma and something new to share who enjoy putting together and delivering a memorable performance, ranging from a thirty-minute inspirational keynote address to a whole-day training event (covering a specialist topic, such as using IT in the classroom, teaching a craft, or running sixth-form workshops for students, such as top revision techniques or how to choose a degree). Work can be sporadic, and earnings in the range of £200–£1,000 per event, depending on numbers attending and the prestige of the event. Most speakers work on a self-employed basis, and may be attached to training companies who organise the conference venue, publicity and delegate registration.

Key roles: performer, entrepreneur, catalyst.

Still interested?

www.osiriseducational.co.uk – Osiris Educational (providers of teacher training courses)

www.dragonfly-training.co.uk – Dragonfly Training (providers of teacher training courses)

www.jla.co.uk – JLA (agency for speakers and conference presenters) www.londonspeakerbureau.com – London Speaker Bureau (speaker and advisory network)

Proofreader

A great fit for teachers interested in making text accurate and readable. The Society for Editors and Proofreaders (SfEP) represents around 600 members. They offer courses including going freelance, proofreading, copy-editing, grammar skills and editing different genres such as fiction and music. If you are freelance you can choose your own working hours, which is great if you value flexibility. Payment is usually per project and you can expect to earn about £10–12 an hour.

Key roles: inspector, writer, communicator.

Still interested?

www.sfep.org.uk – Society for Editors and Proofreaders

Public relations officer

PR officers manage the image and reputation of the organisation they work for or represent a group of clients. Great communication and time management skills underpin this role. You may work across all media formats – writing leaflets, brochures, press releases, speeches, Twitter and web content; attending company events; or speaking on behalf of a company at conferences or fundraising events. Salaries start at around £20,000, rising to £40,000 per annum. You can specialise in politics, good causes, pressure groups or industrial sectors linked to your degree, background or interests.

Key roles: strategist, manager, communicator.

Still interested?

www.cipr.co.uk – Chartered Institute of Public Relations

www.cim.co.uk – Chartered Institute of Marketing

Recruitment consultant

Recruitment consultants usually specialise in one industry. Each has its own jargon, quirks and background knowledge, so education would be a logical starting point for teachers looking to utilise their experience in a different role. The work involves interviewing, placing prospective candidates, liaising with employers, negotiating and meeting targets. Salaries start at around £16,000 and rise to £40,000 plus commission. Entry requirements are more about personal qualities and drive than academic success.

Key roles: manager, entrepreneur, communicator.

Still interested?

www.rec-irp.uk.com – Institute of Recruitment Professionals

www.cipd.co.uk – Chartered Institute of Personnel and Development

Riding therapist

For teachers who love working with horses as much as with children, this could be the ideal job. Being around horses and learning to ride can really boost the confidence and communication skills of children with mild or moderate learning difficulties. Literacy and numeracy can be incorporated into the experiences of being around horses and stables. The Fortune Centre of Riding Therapy requires a teaching qualification, experience in working with children with SEN and a British Horse Society (BHS) horse management qualification.

Key roles: mentor, helper, guide.

Still interested?

www.fortunecentre.org – Fortune Centre of Riding Therapy

www.rda.org.uk – Riding for the Disabled

Sales representative

Perhaps sales reps occupy the Cinderella role within the business world. For each applicant for a sales job, there can be fifty applicants for marketing and advertising posts. You can specialise and sell products, services and ideas that you believe in, perhaps within the world of education. Self-motivated, positive, resilient people happy to work to targets tend to be effective in sales. Basic salaries are often between £15,000 and £20,000 per annum, but if you include commission and on-target earnings (OTE), the salary can double. Most training is in-house.

Key roles: manager, communicator, performer.

Still interested?

www.ismm.co.uk – Institute of Sales and Marketing Management

www.mamsasbp.org.uk – Managing and Marketing Sales Association

Scene of crime officer

Scene of crime officers (SOCOs) attend crime scenes to discover, explore and record evidence. Crimes range from burglary to vehicle theft and, occasionally, murder. SOCOs work with police and are either employed by police services or security companies. Attention to detail is the key requirement. Many skills and techniques are used, including photography and video, to find evidence (such as footprints, tool or weapon marks, and locate tiny fragments of blood, hair, glass or fibre), and you will have to give evidence in court and at post-mortems. Salaries are likely to be between £17,000 and £30,000. Entry requirements are generally at GCSE level. New recruits are trained in-post, and the Crime Scene Investigator (CSI) Learning Programme normally takes twelve months to complete. The many crime scene programmes on TV make this a very sought-after career choice.

Key roles: inspector, explorer, strategist.

Still interested?

www.college.police.uk – College of Policing

School counsellor

Many schools promote experienced staff to be school counsellors, or teachers find that their pastoral role organically grows, eventually replacing teaching classes. Posts in FE and HE are also available. Specialist related jobs in student welfare are more frequent in FE and HE.

Key roles: counsellor, mentor, organiser.

Still interested?

Explore options within your current school, academy chain and local authority.

Schools liaison officer/ administration officer (HE)

The purpose of this role is to promote the general benefits of studying for a degree and to champion the university experience, especially for children likely to be the first in their family to study for a degree. It includes raising the profile of the university in which you are based and its courses. Duties include organising open days, hosting motivational events and conventions, writing publicity material, and recruiting and supervising student mentors. Vacancies are publicised on university vacancy sites. Salaries are generally on administrative scales, though progression to senior posts is possible. Universities are generally big employers, and administration roles reflect this, with specialisms equivalent to all large companies as well as specialist areas such as student recruitment, examinations and accommodation services.

 Key roles: guide, entrepreneur, organiser.

Still interested?

www.aua.ac.uk – Association of University Administrators

Ski instructor/ski guide

If you would like to combine your teaching skills with a hobby and stunning locations (unless you work at a UK-based dry slope), then this could be a good match for you. A number of companies offer instructor training, usually based at a resort in Canada, New Zealand, France or Switzerland, over a period of six to twelve weeks. This costs around £7,500 (inclusive of flights and catered accommodation). Fluency in another language can be useful. Ski guides show experienced skiers around the slopes and help on après-ski activities.

 Earnings are likely to be around £16 per hour. To be an instructor in the UK you need to complete the following training: a skiing or snowboarding level 1 instructor course (which includes 35 hours of practice, which can be done at a UK snowdome) and modules in safeguarding children and first aid, which lead on to a level 2 course.

 Key roles: instructor, performer, trainer.

Still interested?

www.basi.org.uk – British Association of Snowsport Instructors www.snowskool.com – Snow Skool (ski and snowboard courses)

www.alltracksacademy.com – Alltracks Academy (ski and snowboard courses)

Advice from teachers

I was a teacher in London for five years, which I enjoyed, but I lived for my skiing holidays. I now combine both by working as an instructor for six months of the year in Switzerland, at an Outdoor Education Centre in the Lake District for three months and travelling for the other three. I was lucky to buy a house in London when it was possible, which I rent out to finance my current life.

John

Social worker

Social workers work with vulnerable families and individuals to help them make progress in their lives. You will offer emotional and practical support from the initial assessment onwards, and build relationships to liaise with other service providers and professionals. You can specialise in children's services or with other groups in need of support, such as the elderly, people with physical or learning difficulties, people with mental health issues, the homeless, or drug, alcohol or substance abusers.

A qualification approved by the Health and Care Professions Council (HCPC) is required. People without a first degree in social work must take a two-year postgraduate master's degree in social work. Work-based entry routes are also available. Social work is one of the few careers where experience in other working environments and 'life experience' is welcomed prior to entry. Salaries range from £20,000 to £40,000 per annum.

Key roles: helper, advocate, supervisor.

Still interested?

www.skillsforcare.org.uk – Skills for Care

www.basw.co.uk – British Association of Social Workers

Soft play worker

Most towns and industrial estates have a soft play facility offering ball-pits, slides and mini rides for young children to play in and have themed parties. If these are not your idea of a living hell, then you could consider this option. There are opportunities to be creative and introduce new themes and activities. Salaries are likely to start at minimum wage levels, but rise for centre managers who are involved with the business side of the company, including staff recruitment.

Key roles: carer, supervisor, inspector.

Still interested?

To identify vacancies, visit your local facility and ask how positions are advertised.

Solicitor

Solicitors provide professional expert legal advice to individuals, groups or organisations. They usually specialise in one area of law, such as property, wills and probate, divorce and family, personal injury, human rights or commercial disputes. The work combines (1) being able to communicate, negotiate and advocate on behalf of a wide range of people and (2) meticulous research and organisational skills. Training is a lengthy process, but graduates from all degree subjects are welcome to apply to a one-year full-time law conversion course, Graduate Diploma in Law (GDL) or Common Professional Examination (CPE). You then move on to a Legal Practice Course (LPC) over one or two years, which is studied as you work as a trainee solicitor, and also complete a Professional Skills Course (PSC) in order to qualify as a solicitor. Salaries during training can be as low as minimum wage levels. Qualified solicitors can expect to earn between £25,000 and £75,000 per annum. Partners in large firms can earn over £100,000. High salaries can mean twelve-hour shifts and weekend working during busy periods, but most teachers will have experience in this area!

Key roles: manager, advocate, guide.

Still interested?

www.lawsociety.org.uk – Law Society

www.sra.org.uk – Solicitors Regulation Authority

Speech and language therapist

Speech and language therapists (SALTs) support children, adults and the elderly with speech, language and communication issues arising from congenital disorders, strokes or trauma.

Treatment plans can involve family members as well as the patient. The work often involves slow progress and can be very rewarding, as relationships with patients are built. The NHS salary scales go from £21,500 to £28,000. Senior posts can attract salaries up to £40,000 per annum. For most teaching graduates, an approved two-year conversion course will be required. Tuition fees are paid by the NHS and student bursaries are usually available, although competition for places is fierce.

 Key roles: healer, helper, manager.

(i) Still interested?

www.rcslt.org – Royal College of Speech and Language Therapists

www.nhsbsa.nhs.uk – NHS Business Services Authority

Sports coach

Teachers with a talent for a specific sport have the opportunity to develop it into a career option teaching individuals or groups.

(K) Key roles: instructor, guide, mentor.

(i) Still interested?

www.sportscoachuk.org – Sports Coach UK

Surveyor

Surveying offers both a variety and a number of opportunities. Surveyors specialise in one of three areas. All liaise with a wide range of professionals and need project management skills. All write technical reports and advise on legal matters. Building surveyors generally work with planners, renovators and property developers using preventative measures to keep buildings in good condition or suggesting restorative measures.

Commercial/residential surveyors assess and value commercial and residential buildings. Quantity surveyors prepare inventories, plans, feasibility studies, contracts and budgets.

Work is available in private practice, civil service, charities, housing associations, property development, construction and utility companies. Not all teachers will possess a relevant first degree (such as economics, maths, geography or engineering), but postgraduate qualifications with two to three years of vocational experience can be a viable entry route. Salaries start at around £18,000, rising to £30,000 per annum. Partners can earn over £70,000 per annum.

Key roles: strategist, manager, communicator.

Still interested?

www.rics.org – Royal Institution of Chartered Surveyors

www.ciob.org – Chartered Institute of Building

www.cbuilde.com – Chartered Association of Building Engineers

Job area: Teaching English as a Foreign Language (TEFL) see also page 150

⬤ (Senior) teacher

⬤ Teacher centre manager

⬤ Project manager

⬤ Teacher trainer

⬤ Exam services manager/test production/examiner

Exams and tests in the English language are offered to over three million students in over 90 countries across the world each year. The British Council employs over a thousand people to support its work. Jobs are based around the development and production of tests, or the operational management and delivery of the tests. Administrative skills, attention to detail and integrity are at the heart of this work, which can be a natural progression for EFL teachers.

Fluency in the local language can be beneficial.

 Key roles: communicator, organiser, trainer.

 Still interested?

www.britishcouncil.org – British Council

Tour guide

 Tour guides show or escort people around places of interest, such as historic buildings, gardens, towns or regions. Leading tours to exotic locations is possible for more experienced guides. Speaking other languages, good communication, storytelling skills and a memory for facts are usually more important than qualifications. If you have a particular interest you should contact the place directly or research the National Trust, Historic Houses Association, Visit Britain or World Federation of Tourist Guide Associations.

You could also consider setting up your own tour based around a place you love like Oxford or Middlesbrough, an interest you have like ghost walks or a spoof comedy walk.

 Key roles: guide, performer, organiser.

 Still interested?

www.itg.org.uk – Institute of Tourist Guiding

www.aptg.org.uk – London's Association of Professional Tourist Guides

Trade union representative

Reps work to raise the profile of teaching, represent and advise members, and campaign for better schools, pensions, resources and conditions for teachers in schools, colleges and universities. Salaries are equivalent to main teaching scales.

You could also consider working for unions outside the teaching profession. The Trades Union Congress (TUC) runs training courses covering advocacy skills, industrial tribunals, employment law, and health and safety. There are posts in policy-making, research and development, marketing and fundraising. You could even work in the Tolpuddle Martyrs Museum shop!

Key roles: advocate, organiser, communicator.

Still interested?

www.tuc.org.uk – Trades Union Congress

www.teachers.org.uk – National Union of Teachers (NUT)

www.voicetheunion.org.uk – Voice

www.atl.org.uk – Association of Teachers and Lecturers (ATL)

www.nasuwt.org.uk – National Association of Schoolmasters/ Union of Women Teachers (NASUWT)

Train driver

This is a dream job for many eight-year-olds! Train drivers are responsible for moving passengers or freight across the rail network. As well as the obvious, the work involves checking equipment and liaising with control centres and passengers. Drivers can expect to earn between £30,000 and £60,000 per annum, following an initial training period of up to eighteen months. Good general fitness, awareness of safety/emergency procedures and excellent concentration are essential attributes.

Other roles including signalling, maintenance, project management and management may also appeal.

Key roles: inspector, protector, explorer.

Still interested?

www.careersthatmove.co.uk – Careers That Move

www.networkrail.co.uk – Network Rail

www.atoc.org – Association of Train Operating Companies

Training officer

The roles of training officer and teacher overlap in the delivery of training to groups of adults. Training officers also have to organise external providers by researching training needs (linked to company goals), budgeting, commissioning trainers and evaluating the impact of training. Salaries are similar to the teaching scale. Additional qualifications are available. Teaching adults is more like teaching children than most teachers expect!

Key roles: trainer, communicator, strategist.

Still interested?

www.cipd.co.uk – Chartered Institute of Personnel and Development

Visitor attraction manager

Tourism is an economic growth area, resulting in good prospects within this sector. As a manager of a theme park, zoo, sanctuary, heritage site, landmark or museum collection (from lawnmowers to pencils), you would be responsible for maximising visitor numbers and ensuring visitors have a pleasant experience. The varied work is likely to include management duties such as budgeting, staff recruitment and development, health and safety, and marketing/advertising your attraction. If you have SLT experience at a larger school, this is likely to be a good grounding for this type of work, where leadership, organisational and communication skills (plus energy and enthusiasm) are essential. Salaries are likely to be equivalent to the main teaching scale, except in smaller attractions. Qualifications in cultural venue operations, hospitality and tourism management are available. You could contact the attractions directly to check out their recruitment procedures or organise a school visit to suss out the place. See the Association of Leading Visitor Attractions (ALVA) for ideas and to search for organisations that match your own interests.

Key roles: manager, entrepreneur, communicator.

Still interested?

www.hospitalityguild.co.uk – Hospitality Guild

www.cthawards.com – Confederation of Tourism and Hospitality

www.alva.org.uk – Association of Leading Visitor Attractions

Voiceover artist

Voiceover artists record adverts for radio and TV, content for websites, computer games, and even high-end cartoons and movies. Voice actors on *The Simpsons* reportedly earn around £200,000 per episode. They have control of their voice, are confident and are comfortable performing – traits developed and honed by teachers on a daily basis. The entry route usu-

ally starts with recording your voice. Email the recording to studios and agents, and wait for an orderly queue to form for your services … Opportunities also exist for providing audio description work on films and TV programmes.

Key roles: performer, improviser, comedian.

Still interested?

www.voice123.com – Voice 123 (a marketplace to find professional voice actors)

www.edgestudio.com – Edge Studio (voiceover education and production)

Volunteer organiser

Volunteer organisers recruit, train and manage unpaid volunteers. The ability to communicate clearly with a wide range of people is key to success in this role. You are likely to be employed by charities (such as Barnardo's, the British Heart Foundation, Scope), hospitals, museums, social services and specialist event companies (such as those organising music festivals and sporting/cultural occasions). If you have a connection to the organisation you are likely to find the work very rewarding. Salaries are likely to range between £20,000 and £30,000 per annum.

Key roles: communicator, organiser, catalyst.

Still interested?

www.volunteermanagers.org.uk – Association of Volunteer Managers

www.volunteering.org.uk – National Council for Voluntary Organisations (NCVO)

Worker with adults with special needs

Building the skills, confidence and self-worth of adults as a tutor in a community education centre or college can be very rewarding work. Some providers offer residential and respite places. Instructors and day centre workers work individually and with groups. They can work alongside professionals such as social workers, nurses and therapists. They can lead activities such as cooking, painting, games and craft activities. Interpersonal and communication skills are required. Centres are LA-run or funded by charities. An online directory of colleges can be used to identify potential employers in any geographical location.

Key roles: carer, advocate, helper.

Still interested?

www.natspec.org.uk – Association of National Specialist Colleges

www.disabilitynow.org.uk – Disability Now

Writer (educational textbooks)

Student study guides, educational books and other resources, including those online, are often written by experienced teachers. Are there any books you would like to write? Explore the shelves of your local bookshop or conduct a search on Amazon to identify a gap and, if you see one, contact publishers of similar books with a proposal. Each publisher has their own preferred way of being contacted. Check their website to ensure you adhere to their rules for submission of ideas. Income is usually 10% of book sales. Most writers combine their writing with other income streams, such as giving talks and presentations based around the content of their book. Some educational writers do break through into the mass market, such as Ken Robinson and Gervase Phinn.

Key roles: writer, instructor, creator.

Still interested?

Educational publishers' websites will list details of their submissions procedure. Publishers include Bloomsbury, Macmillan, McGraw-Hill and Wiley.

www.jobs.ac.uk/careers-advice/working-in-higher-education/1868/academic-writing-how-to-write-a-textbook
– article on how to write an academic textbook

Youth worker

The aim of the job is helping young people believe in themselves and prepare for life – and work – with confidence. Teachers do this in the classroom, whereas youth workers use activities such as sport, drama and the arts to confront issues like crime, drugs, health and bullying. Youth workers meet young people in the places where they congregate, such as parks and shopping areas. Building trust and offering personal support to teenagers is the core of the work. Like teaching and all work with children, being able to build a rapport, respect, resilience, initiative and patience are essential skills. Traditionally people enter youth work as volunteers or as youth support workers. Professional posts will require a Joint Negotiating Committee (JNC) recognised degree or postgraduate qualification. A list of validated courses is available on the National Youth Agency (NYA) website. Salaries are around £25,000 per annum. Many people work part-time or on a self-employed basis.

 Key roles: mentor, improviser, leader.

Still interested?

www.byc.org.uk – British Youth Council

www.nya.org.uk – National Youth Agency

Finally ...

> If you think education is expensive, try ignorance.
>
> attributed to Robert Orben

How to better manage your career (and life)

Below is the list of beliefs presented at the start of this book – the beliefs you can adopt to manage your career positively and proactively.

How are you doing now? Better than you were at the start? The more of these beliefs you've adopted, the better.

They will help you be successful – but if you want to be even more popular, you could share them with others and help them progress too.

1   I know my skills and what I'm good at.   ◯

....

2   I know the skills I need to develop.   ◯

....

3   I can do an elevator pitch (a thirty-second summary of my   ◯
    skills and best achievements to date, showcasing what I
    can add to an organisation or team).

....

4   I keep a record of all my major achievements at work.   ◯

....

5   I seek regular feedback on my performance from colleagues   ◯
    and students.

....

6   I share my ideas with other professionals.   ◯

....

7   I take on new roles, projects or research at work to   ◯
    enhance my skills and experience.

....

8   I feel good about myself at work.   ◯

....

9   I know what opportunities for progression are available in   ◯
    my current school.

....

10 I'm aware of the politics, tensions and 'characters' in my   ◯
    current school.

....

11 I'm aware of the career options available to teachers in the UK and abroad. ◯

....

12 I'm aware of the job options available outside teaching, and the entry routes for these options. ◯

....

13 I have a pretty clear idea of my career direction, and what/where I'd like to be in three years' time. ◯

....

14 I have discussed my career plan with important people in my life. ◯

....

15 I'm content with my life outside work. ◯

....

16 I have a life outside work. ◯

....

17 I have mentors. ◯

....

18 I am articulate and assertive. ◯

....

19 I keep up to date with what's going on by reading articles, blogs, journals, newspapers and books about education and my subject specialism. ◯

....

20 I review and reflect on my progress. ◯

....

Thinking about where you are now

1   I know my skills and what I'm good at.   ....

2   I know the skills I need to develop.   ....

3   I can do an elevator pitch.   ....

4   I keep a record of all my major achievements at work.   ....

5   I seek regular feedback on my performance from colleagues and students.   ....

6   I share my ideas with other professionals.   ....

7   I take on new roles, projects or research at work to enhance my skills and experience.   ....

▶ Do you know how to develop your skills further? Can you show that you have these qualities? Part 1 of this book was aimed at helping you clarify your skills and strengths.

▶ You should now have a plan, and a list of skills to help you within your current role and to prepare you for your future career aspirations.

▶ This is a good way to check that you are aware of who you are, what you have achieved and what you can contribute. Has this pitch changed from the one you did at the start of this book? It is important to be able to define ourselves by more than our job title. How do you introduce yourself at a party? 'I'm a maths teacher,' or 'I motivate and inspire children to believe in themselves and be lifelong learners'?

▶ Have you added to this list recently? If not, that's a big clue that your current role is not helping you develop.

▶ What have you learned from the feedback you have sought? What does it tell you about your next six months?

▶ Connecting to like-minded people is really important. Networking can reignite your passion and commitment to teaching or help you realise your future lies elsewhere. Networking is perhaps the best way to find your niche.

▶ Has this helped you spot new opportunities or skills you weren't aware you had?

8 I feel good about myself at work.   ·····························◁

9 I know what opportunities for progression are   ·····························◁
   available in my current school.

10 I'm aware of the politics, tensions and 'characters' in ·····························◁
   my current school.

11 I'm aware of the career options available to teachers   ·····························◁
   in the UK and abroad.

12 I'm aware of the job options available outside   ·····························◁
   teaching and the entry routes for these options.

13 I have a pretty clear idea of my career direction, and   ·····························◁
   what/where I'd like to be in three years' time.

14 I have discussed my career plan with important   ·····························◁
   people in my life.

15 I'm content with my life outside work.   ·····························◁

16 I have a life outside work.   ·····························◁

▶ What has changed now you've explored your skills and the options open to you outside teaching?

▶ This should be clearer. Are you now aware how you can move your career forward?

▶ Teachers who can identify these factors are better placed to navigate their way through some of the manoeuvring – or avoid it completely.

▶ You should now have a better idea of the options available to you. If not, revisit Part 2 of this book.

▶ Are you aware of your strengths and transferable skills, and how you could apply these in alternative careers? Which jobs in Part 3 appeal to you?

▶ This book is designed to help you with this.

▶ Have you discussed your progress as you've read this book? What feedback have they given you?

▶ If there are areas that need to be improved, start to list these and do something about them. Small steps are best. You can start to change things like health and fitness in small ways. Finding a new place to live or a new partner may be more complicated.

▶ Having friends and being socially connected are crucial for human happiness. If you're not yet ready or able to change career, focusing on other aspects of your life, like friendships and hobbies, could be a positive first step.

17 I have mentors. ....

18 I am articulate and assertive. ....

19 I keep up to date with what's going on by reading ....
   articles, blogs, journals, newspapers and books
   about education and my subject specialism.

20 I review and reflect on my progress. ....

▶ This should be in addition to friends, family and allocated line managers. Have you already identified people who can help you, and made contact with them?

▶ Are you clearer about your next step? Identify at least three things you can do within the next week that will move you forward.

▶ If you haven't discovered the joy of blogs, a quick web search will guide you to the current trending blogs.

▶ What is your next move? What will you be doing in the next week, month or year to ensure you continue to make progress?

Knowledge-doubling curve

The architect and inventor Buckminster Fuller estimated that human knowledge doubled approximately every century up to 1900. Today it doubles each year. Soon, what we collectively know is forecast to double every twelve hours![5] The impact this has on teaching has only just begun to be felt. Jobs are evolving too and we must be vigilant to ensure we don't miss out. For example:

Cloud architect

There was a statistic widely quoted by careers advisers a few years ago which claimed that 50% of all jobs available and advertised in ten years' time haven't been invented yet. This book will thus be missing many exciting new opportunities that are yet to emerge. 'Cloud architect' is included here to remind us to keep a look-out for new opportunities. Most of the hidden jobs have already been invented, but they are difficult to track and narrow down. That's the focus of this book. We all need to be vigilant and continually look out for opportunities. Think of cloud architect as your ideal job: it is waiting for you to discover it – it won't come to you.

Cloud architects are involved with storing information – not on a physical drive you keep (or lose), but in a virtual place (the cloud) where it can't be lost. The information is also stored physically in big warehouses somewhere. Job adverts for these posts request experience of: .Net, particularly Microsoft Azure and/or Java, Python, Perl, PHP Web Services, RESTful, SOAP, Agile software development, UML, object-orientated programming, Hibernate, MyBatis, Ruby on Rails and Scala. If you read

---

5   See David Russell Schilling, Knowledge doubling every 12 months, soon to be every 12 hours, *Industry Tap* (19 April 2013). Available at: www.industrytap.com/knowledge-doubling-every-12-months-soon-to-be-every-12-hours/3950.

the list and suddenly feel old, wondering if they're tracks from Orchestral Manoeuvres in the Dark albums, don't worry – some ads also ask for innovation skills and vision, communication, negotiation, leadership and project management skills and technical proficiency. Most jobs require these two skill sets: technical/up-to-date stuff that's forever evolving and people/human/communication/persuasion skills (which have been in demand since fledgling human societies started trading goods). As a teacher, you have a good claim on the latter skill set. The former is probably something in which you've harboured an interest for a long time.

Key roles: inventor, improviser, manager.

Still interested?

Keep your eyes and ears open to new opportunities.

Unusual jobs

If you haven't found anything in this book that appeals to you, I'll have one more attempt by sharing a list of some of the most unusual jobs advertised over the past year:

Sea-lion trainer	Bounty hunter
Dog food taster	Human scarecrow
Lego sculptor	Luxury house-sitter
Dog yoga teacher/dog surfing instructor	
Nude cruise worker	
Undercover bridesmaid	
Professional mourner	
Iceberg mover	
Chicken sexer	

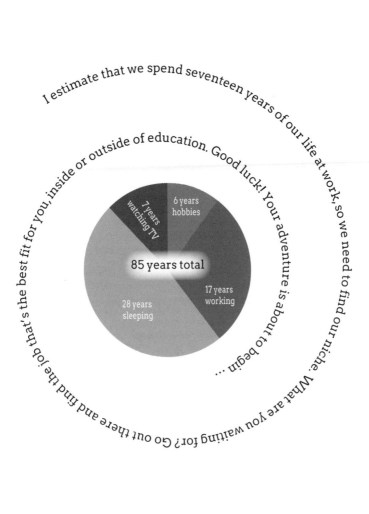

I estimate that we spend seventeen years of our life at work, so we need to find our niche. Your adventure is about to begin ... What are you waiting for? Go out there and find the job that's the best fit for you, inside or outside of education. Good luck!

6 years hobbies

7 years watching TV

85 years total

17 years working

28 years sleeping

Appendix

Further information

Trade unions

Trade unions can be fantastic resources to assist your career development. They run courses, events, conferences and seminars. The CPD offered ranges from classroom strategies to leadership. The main unions are listed below.

www.unison.org.uk – UNISON

www.teachers.org.uk – National Union of Teachers (NUT)

www.nasuwt.org.uk – National Association of Schoolmasters/ Union of Women Teachers (NASUWT)

www.atl.org.uk – Association of Teachers and Lecturers (ATL)

www.edapt.org.uk – Edapt

www.voicetheunion.org.uk – Voice

www.naht.org.uk – National Association of Head Teachers (NAHT)

Websites

Some of the best and most useful websites for careers guidance are listed below.

https://getintoteaching.education.gov.uk – Department for Education (jobs and information on funding, bursaries, training routes into teaching and teaching events)

www.theguardian.com/education – *Guardian* Education

www.tes.com – *TES*

www.eteach.com – Eteach (teaching jobs across the UK and abroad)

www.lgjobs.com – Local Government Jobs

www.voice-online.co.uk, www.allthetopbananas.com/voice and www.opportunities.co.uk – jobs

Bibliography

ATL (2016) Workload drives the teacher recruitment and retention crisis, new survey finds (4 April). Available at: www.atl.org.uk/media-office/2016/workload-drives-the-teacher-recruitment-and-retention-crisis.asp.

Banning-Lover, Rachel (2016) 60-hour weeks and unrealistic targets: teachers' working lives uncovered, *The Guardian* (22 March). Available at: www.theguardian.com/teacher-network/datablog/2016/mar/22/60-hour-weeks-and-unrealistic-targets-teachers-working-lives-uncovered.

Branham, Leigh (2005) *The 7 Hidden Reasons Employees Leave: How to Recognise the Subtle Signs and Act Before It's Too Late*. New York: AMACOM.

Brighouse, Tim (2007) *How Successful Head Teachers Survive and Thrive*. (Abingdon: RM Education).

Campbell, Joseph (2008) *The Hero with a Thousand Faces*, Bollingen Series XVII, 3rd edn. Novato, CA: New World Library.

Carney, Mark (2016) The Spectre of Monetarism (Roscoe Lecture) speech given by Mark Carney, at Liverpool John Moores University, 5 December. Available at: www.bankofengland.co.uk/publications/Documents/speeches/2016/speech946.pdf.

Clarke, Marilyn (2009) Plodders, pragmatists, visionaries and opportunists: career patterns and employability, *Career Development International*, 14(1): 8–28.

Coe, Robert, Aloisi, Cesare, Higgins, Steve and Major, Lee Elliot (2014) *What Makes Great Teaching? Review of the Underpinning Research*. London: Sutton Trust. Available at: www.suttontrust.com/wp-content/uploads/2014/10/What-Makes-Great-Teaching-REPORT.pdf.

Dilts, Robert (1990) *Changing Belief Systems with NLP*. Capitola, CA: Meta Publications.

Earley, Peter and Weindling, Dick (2007) Do school leaders have a shelf life? Career stages and headteacher performance, *Educational Management, Administration and Leadership*, 35(1): 73–88.

Greene, Peter (2015) A not quitting letter, *Curmudgucation* [blog] (4 November). Available at: http://curmudgucation. blogspot.co.uk/2015/11/a-not-quitting-letter.html.

GTI Media (2016) *The Guardian UK 300*: the largest employer ranking careers product on campus. Available at: http:// gtimedia.co.uk/work/products/guardian-uk-300/2016-17.

Hawkins, Peter (1999) *The Art of Building Windmills: Career Tactics for the 21st Century.* Liverpool: Graduate Into Employment Unit, University of Liverpool.

Hill, Napoleon (2009 [1937]) *Think and Grow Rich*. Chichester: Capstone.

Hoggard, Liz (2007) *How to be Happy*. London: BBC Books.

King, Stephen (2000) *On Writing: A Memoir of the Craft*. London: Hodder and Stoughton.

Knapton, Sarah (2015) Five things you can do to be happier right now, *The Telegraph* (31 May). Available at: www. telegraph.co.uk/culture/hay-festival/11640753/Five-things-you-can-do-to-be-happier-right-now.html.

Lencioni, Patrick (2015) *The Truth About Employee Engagement: A Fable About Addressing the Three Root Causes of Job Misery*. San Francisco, CA: Jossey-Bass.

Lightfoot, Liz (2016a) Nearly half of England's teachers plan to leave in next five years, *The Guardian* (22 March). Available at: www.theguardian.com/education/2016/mar/22/ teachers-plan-leave-five-years-survey-workload-england.

Lightfoot, Liz (2016b) Tips on reducing teacher stress from the 'happiest school on earth', *The Guardian* (22 March). Available at: www.theguardian.com/education/2016/mar/22/ teaching-crisis-school-what-keep-them.

Luscombe, Belinda (2010) Do we need $75,000 a year to be happy? *Time* (6 September). Available at: http://content.time.com/time/magazine/article/0,9171,2019628,00.html.

Press Gazette (2015) *How to be a Journalist 2015/16*. London: Press Gazette in association with the National Council for the Training of Journalists. Available at: https://issuu.com/press_gazette/docs/trainingguidefinal_hires_p5_v3.

Robinson, Ken (2006) Do schools kill creativity? *TED.com* [video]. Available at: www.ted.com/talks/ken_robinson_says_schools_kill_creativity?language=en.

Russell, Bertrand (2006[1930]) *The Conquest of Happiness*. Abingdon: Routledge Classics.

Schilling, David Russell (2013) Knowledge doubling every 12 months, soon to be every 12 hours, *Industry Tap* (19 April). Available at: www.industrytap.com/knowledge-doubling-every-12-months-soon-to-be-every-12-hours/3950.

Seligman, Martin E. P. (2002) *Authentic Happiness: Using the New Positive Psychology to Realize Your Potential for Lasting Fulfillment*. New York: Free Press.

Wagner, Tony and Dintersmith, Ted (2015) *Most Likely to Succeed: Preparing Our Kids for the Innovation Era*. New York: Simon & Schuster.

Waldinger, Robert (2016) What makes a good life? Lessons from the longest study on happiness, *TED.com* [video]. Available at: www.ted.com/talks/robert_waldinger_what_makes_a_good_life_lessons_from_the_longest_study_on_happiness/transcript?language=en.

Watts, Alan (1951) *The Wisdom of Insecurity*. New York: Pantheon Books.

Wheale, Sally (2015) Four in 10 new teachers quit within a year, *The Guardian* (31 March). Available at: www.theguardian.com/education/2015/mar/31/four-in-10-new-teachers-quit-within-a-year.